TREASURY OF LITERATURE

Sea of Wonder

SENIOR AUTHORS
ROGER C. FARR
DOROTHY S. STRICKLAND

AUTHORS
RICHARD F. ABRAHAMSON
ELLEN BOOTH CHURCH
BARBARA BOWEN COULTER
BERNICE E. CULLINAN
MARGARET A. GALLEGO
W. DORSEY HAMMOND
JUDITH L. IRVIN
KAREN KUTIPER
DONNA M. OGLE
TIMOTHY SHANAHAN
PATRICIA SMITH
JUNKO YOKOTA
HALLIE KAY YOPP

SENIOR CONSULTANTS
ASA G. HILLIARD III
JUDY M. WALLIS

CONSULTANTS
ALONZO A. CRIM
ROLANDO R. HINOJOSA-SMITH
LEE BENNETT HOPKINS
ROBERT J. STERNBERG

HARCOURT BRACE & COMPANY
Orlando Atlanta Austin Boston San Francisco Chicago Dallas New York
Toronto London

ISBN 0-15-301253-6

 2345678910 048 97 96 95 94

Acknowledgments

For permission to reprint copyrighted material, grateful acknowledgment is made to the following sources:

Bradbury Press, an Affiliate of Macmillan, Inc.: From *Crinkleroot's Book of Animal Tracking* by Jim Arnosky. Copyright © 1989 by Jim Arnosky. From *The News About Dinosaurs* by Patricia Lauber. Text copyright © 1989 by Patricia Lauber.

The Ciardi Family Publishing Trust: "Rain Sizes" from *The Reason for the Pelican* by John Ciardi. Text copyright 1959 by John Ciardi.

Crown Publishers, Inc.: From pp. 34–55 in *The Secret of the Seal* by Deborah L. Davis, illustrated by Judy Labrasca. Text copyright © 1989 by Deborah L. Davis; illustrations copyright © 1989 by Judy Labrasca. From *Animal Fact/Animal Fable* by Seymour Simon, cover illustration by Diane de Groat. Text copyright © 1979 by Seymour Simon; cover illustration copyright © 1979 by Diane de Groat.

Dell Books, a division of Bantam Doubleday Dell Publishing Group, Inc.: The Pizza Monster by Marjorie W. Sharmat and Mitchell Sharmat, illustrated by Denise Brunkus. Text copyright © 1989 by Marjorie Weinman Sharmat and Mitchell Sharmat; illustrations copyright © 1989 by Denise Brunkus. Cover illustration by Denise Brunkus from *The Sly Spy* by Marjorie and Mitchell Sharmat. Illustration copyright © 1990 by Denise Brunkus.

Dial Books for Young Readers, a division of Penguin Books USA Inc.: Bringing the Rain to Kapiti Plain by Verna Aardema, illustrated by Beatriz Vidal. Text copyright © 1981 by Verna Aardema; illustrations copyright © 1981 by Beatriz Vidal. *The Patchwork Quilt* by Valerie Flournoy, illustrated by Jerry Pinkney. Text copyright © 1985 by Valerie Flournoy; illustrations copyright © 1985 by Jerry Pinkney.

Doubleday, a division of Bantam Doubleday Dell Publishing Group, Inc.: From *Why Can't I Fly?* by Ken Brown. Copyright © 1991 by Ken Brown.

Farrar, Straus and Giroux, Inc.: "Seal" from *Laughing Time* by William Jay Smith. Text copyright © 1955, 1957, 1980, 1990 by William Jay Smith.

Greenwillow Books, a division of William Morrow & Company, Inc.: "I Am Flying" from *The New Kid on the Block* by Jack Prelutsky. Text copyright © 1984 by Jack Prelutsky. "Rainy Rainy Saturday" from *Rainy Rainy Saturday* by Jack Prelutsky, cover illustration by Marylin Hafner. Text copyright © 1980 by Jack Prelutsky; cover illustration copyright © 1980 by Marylin Hafner.

Harcourt Brace & Company: Cover illustration from *The Magic Fan* by Keith Baker. Copyright © 1989 by Keith Baker. *The Armadillo from Amarillo* by Lynne Cherry. Copyright © 1994 by Lynne Cherry. Stamp designs copyright © by United States Postal Service. Reproduction of images courtesy of Gilbert Palmer, the National Aeronautics and Space Administration, the Austin News Agency, Festive Enterprises, Jack Lewis/Texas Department of Transportation, the Baxter Lane Company, Wyco Colour Productions, Frank Burd, and City Sights. Cover illustration by Leo Politi from *Lorenzo the Naughty Parrot* by Tony Johnston. Illustration copyright © 1992 by Leo Politi. Pronunciation Key from *HBJ School Dictionary*, Third Edition. Text copyright © 1990 by Harcourt Brace & Company.

HarperCollins Publishers: Sunken Treasure by Gail Gibbons. Copyright © 1988 by Gail Gibbons. "Tradition" from *Under the Sunday Tree* by Eloise Greenfield, paintings by Amos Ferguson. Text copyright © 1988 by Eloise Greenfield; paintings copyright © 1988 by Amos Ferguson.

Holiday House, Inc.: From *Yellowstone Fires: Flames and Rebirth* by Dorothy Hinshaw Patent. Text copyright © 1990 by Dorothy Hinshaw Patent.

Henry Holt and Company, Inc.: Cover illustration from *In the Eyes of the Cat: Japanese Poetry for All Seasons*, selected and illustrated by Demi, translated by Tze-si Huang. Copyright © 1992 by Demi.

Houghton Mifflin Company: Cover illustration from *No Such Things* by Bill Peet. Copyright © 1969 by William Peet. *The Wreck of the Zephyr* by Chris Van Allsburg. Copyright © 1983 by Chris Van Allsburg.

Alfred A. Knopf, Inc.: Song and Dance Man by Karen Ackerman, illustrated by Stephen Gammell. Text copyright © 1988 by Karen Ackerman; illustrations copyright © 1988 by Stephen Gammell. "A Day When Frogs Wear Shoes" from *More Stories Julian Tells* by Ann Cameron, illustrated by Ann Strugnell. Text copyright © 1986 by Ann Cameron; illustrations copyright © 1986 by Ann Strugnell. Cover illustration by Thomas B. Allen from *In Coal Country* by Judith Hendershot. Illustration copyright © 1987 by Thomas B. Allen. "April Rain Song" from *Selected Poems of Langston Hughes* by Langston Hughes. Text copyright 1932 by Alfred A. Knopf, Inc., renewed 1960 by Langston Hughes.

continued on page 352

Dear Reader,

Our world is full of wonders, from a treasure half-hidden on the ocean floor to the secret life of dinosaurs. In *Sea of Wonder,* you will read about frogs wearing shoes, about pizza monsters, and about a space shuttle with an armadillo on board. You might be a little surprised by all the wondrous things you'll see in the pages that follow.

You'll visit some new, exciting places, too. Walk on an African plain hoping for rain, or watch over a seal with an Inuit friend. Look through William Muñoz's camera lens to witness the drama of a major forest fire. Share the wonder of a patchwork quilt and the tales it tells about family life.

As you read the stories in this book, think about the special people you meet. Eloise Greenfield talks about how we learn from one another. She says:

> . . . knowledge came from other lands
> Africans of long ago
> passed it down to us and so
> now we pass it on to you . . .

The wonderful literature in this book was passed on to us, and we are proud to pass it on to you.

Sincerely,
The Authors

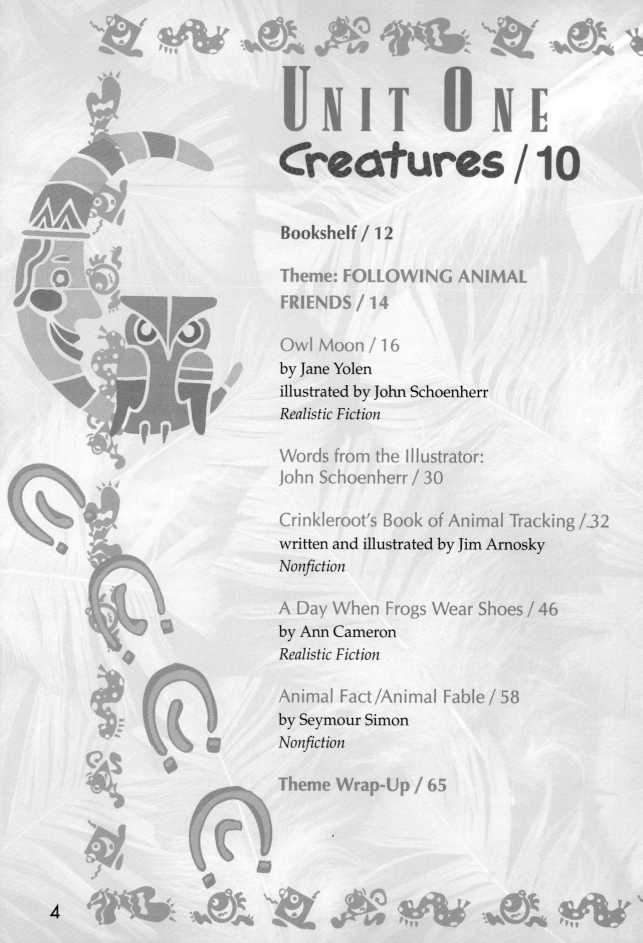

UNIT ONE
Creatures / 10

UNIT TWO
Puzzlers / 120

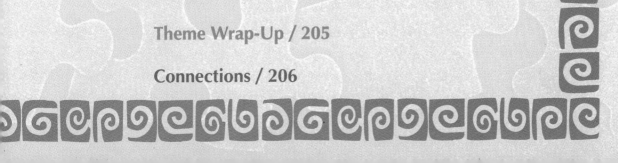

U n i t T h r e e
Memories / 208

9

UNIT ONE

Creatures

Whether you observe owls in a nearby field or seals in Alaska, noticing clues can tell you a great deal about animals. By looking at the sculptures of the Inuits of Canada, who call themselves "the first people," you can learn about animals in their environment. As you read these selections, watch for clues that tell about animals and the way they live.

THEMES

BOOKSHELF 33

ANIMAL FACT/ANIMAL FABLE

by Seymour Simon

Are bats really blind? Why do dogs wag their tails? This book looks at some common beliefs about animals and separates fact from fable.

Award-Winning Author

Harcourt Brace Library Book

THE STORIES JULIAN TELLS

by Ann Cameron

Each of these six short stories about Julian, his friends, and his family will be sure to bring lots of smiles and laughs. They're as much fun to read silently as they are to read aloud.

ALA Notable Book, Irma Simonton Black Award

Harcourt Brace Library Book

No Such Things

by Bill Peet

This story in rhyme is a collection of some of Bill Peet's craziest creatures. It's an all-time favorite!

Children's Choice

Lorenzo the Naughty Parrot

by Tony Johnston

Lorenzo, a well-meaning parrot, is a watchbird who tries to protect the family he lives with in Mexico. But Lorenzo's love of cookies and his love of getting into trouble lead to some hilarious adventures.

Award-Winning Illustrator

In the Eyes of the Cat

selected and illustrated by Demi

A collection of colorfully illustrated Japanese poetry that includes images of young calves cooling themselves in a stream, a garter snake going in and out of the grass at the same time, and a cat with eyes the same color as the sea.

Award-Winning Illustrator

THEME

Following Animal Friends

Have you ever wondered how animals live every day? These selections will tell you some secrets about animals. The facts are mixed in with the fun.

CONTENTS

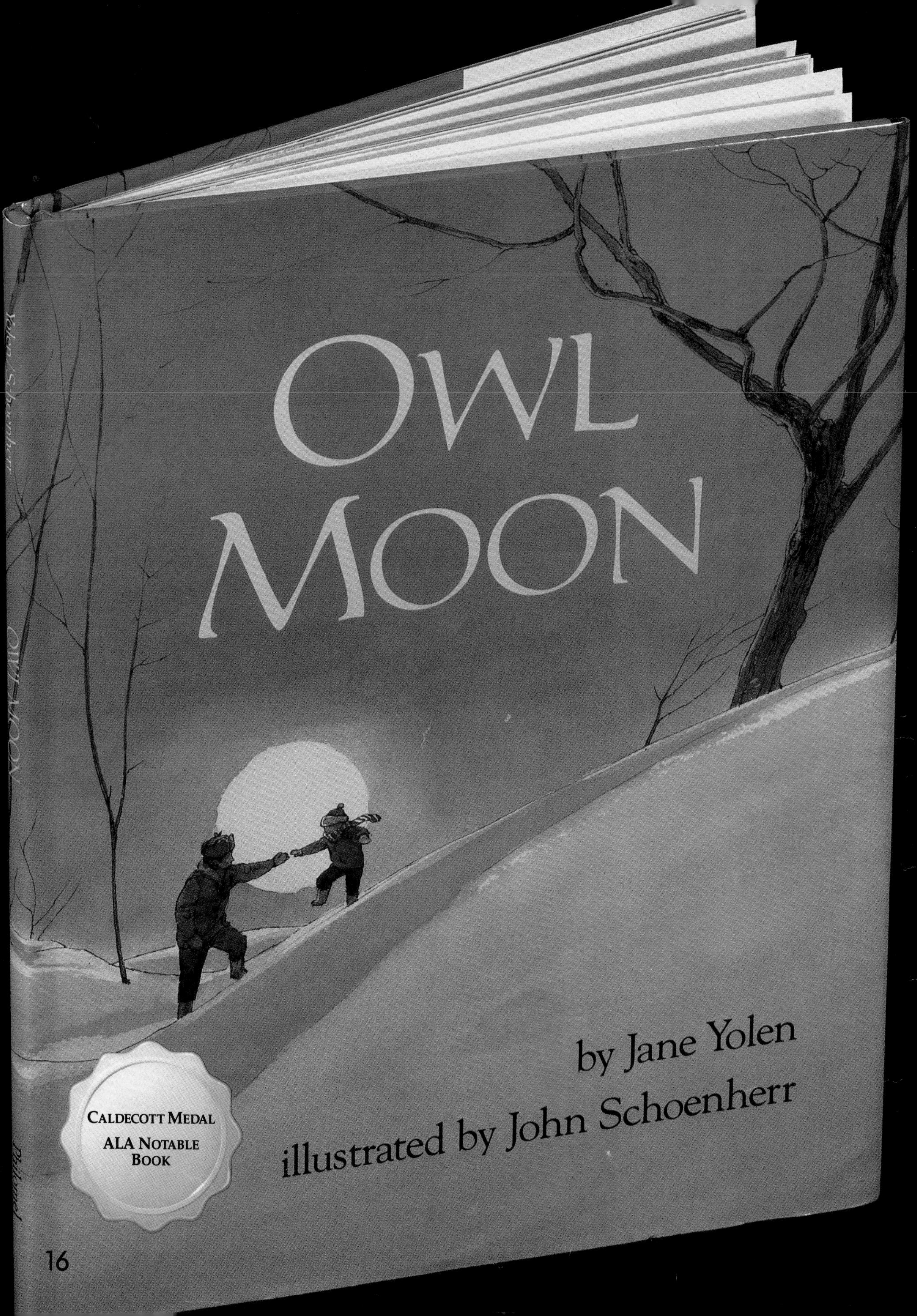
OWL MOON
by Jane Yolen
illustrated by John Schoenherr
CALDECOTT MEDAL
ALA NOTABLE BOOK
Yolen / Schoenherr
OWL MOON
Philomel

It was late one winter night,
long past my bedtime,
when Pa and I went owling.
There was no wind.
The trees stood still
as giant statues.
And the moon was so bright
the sky seemed to shine.
Somewhere behind us
a train whistle blew,
long and low,
like a sad, sad song.

I could hear it
through the woolen cap
Pa had pulled down
over my ears.
A farm dog answered the train,
and then a second dog
joined in.
They sang out,
trains and dogs,
for a real long time.
And when their voices
faded away
it was as quiet as a dream.
We walked on toward the woods,
Pa and I.

Our feet crunched
over the crisp snow
and little gray footprints
followed us.
Pa made a long shadow,
but mine was short and round.
I had to run after him
every now and then
to keep up,
and my short, round shadow
bumped after me.

But I never called out.
If you go owling
you have to be quiet,
that's what Pa always says.

I had been waiting
to go owling with Pa
for a long, long time.

18

We reached the line
of pine trees,
black and pointy
against the sky,
and Pa held up his hand.
I stopped right where I was
and waited.
He looked up,
as if searching the stars,
as if reading a map up there.

The moon made his face
into a silver mask.
Then he called:
"Whoo-whoo-who-who-who-whooooooo,"
the sound of a Great Horned Owl.
"Whoo-whoo-who-who-who-whooooooo."

Again he called out.
And then again.
After each call
he was silent
and for a moment we both listened.
But there was no answer.
Pa shrugged
and I shrugged.
I was not disappointed.
My brothers all said
sometimes there's an owl
and sometimes there isn't.

We walked on.
I could feel the cold,
as if someone's icy hand
was palm-down on my back.
And my nose
and the tops of my cheeks
felt cold and hot
at the same time.
But I never said a word.
If you go owling
you have to be quiet
and make your own heat.

We went into the woods.
The shadows
were the blackest things
I had ever seen.
They stained the white snow.
My mouth felt furry,
for the scarf over it
was wet and warm.
I didn't ask
what kinds of things
hide behind black trees
in the middle of the night.
When you go owling
you have to be brave.

Then we came to a clearing
in the dark woods.
The moon was high above us.
It seemed to fit
exactly
over the center of the clearing
and the snow below it
was whiter than the milk
in a cereal bowl.

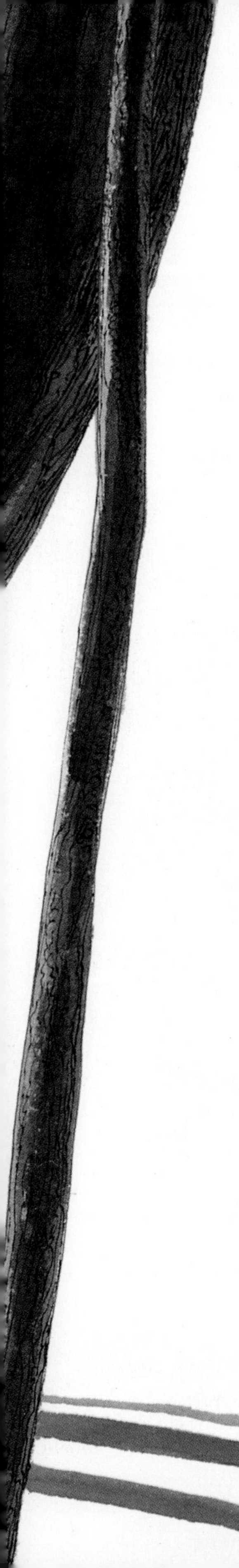

I sighed
and Pa held up his hand
at the sound.
I put my mittens
over the scarf
over my mouth
and listened hard.
And then Pa called:
"*Whoo-whoo-who-who-who-whooooooo.*
Whoo-whoo-who-who-who-whooooooo."
I listened
and looked so hard
my ears hurt
and my eyes got cloudy
with the cold.
Pa raised his face
to call out again,
but before he could
open his mouth
an echo
came threading its way
through the trees.
"*Whoo-whoo-who-who-who-whooooooo.*"

Pa almost smiled.
Then he called back:
"Whoo-whoo-who-who-who-whooooooo,"
just as if he
and the owl
were talking about supper
or about the woods
or the moon
or the cold.
I took my mitten
off the scarf
off my mouth,
and I almost smiled, too.

The owl's call came closer,
from high up in the trees
on the edge of the meadow.
Nothing in the meadow moved.
All of a sudden
an owl shadow,
part of the big tree shadow,
lifted off
and flew right over us.
We watched silently
with heat in our mouths,
the heat of all those words
we had not spoken.
The shadow hooted again.

Pa turned on
his big flashlight
and caught the owl
just as it was landing
on a branch.

For one minute,
three minutes,
maybe even a hundred minutes,
we stared at one another.

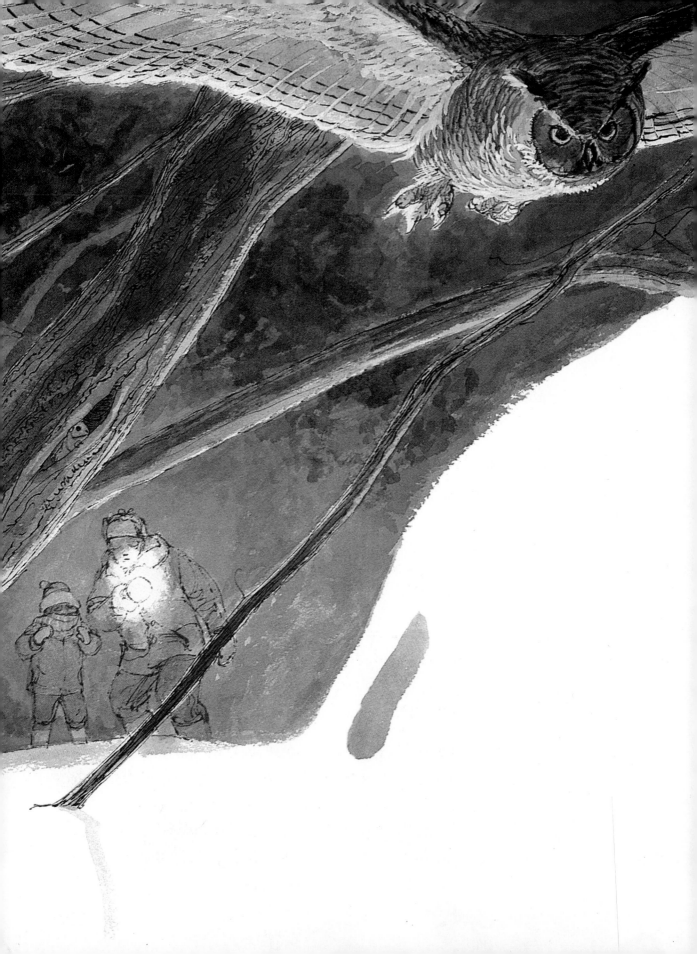

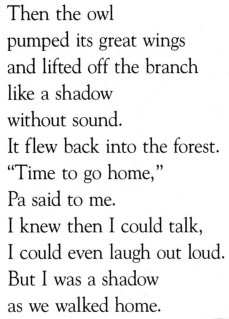

Then the owl
pumped its great wings
and lifted off the branch
like a shadow
without sound.
It flew back into the forest.
"Time to go home,"
Pa said to me.
I knew then I could talk,
I could even laugh out loud.
But I was a shadow
as we walked home.

When you go owling
you don't need words
or warm
or anything but hope.
That's what Pa says.
The kind of hope
that flies
on silent wings
under a shining
Owl Moon.

If you could be any character in this
story, which would you be? Why?

According to the story, what is the most
important thing to take with you when
you go owling? Share the reasons for your
choice.

WRITE The child tells us that "sometimes
there's an owl and sometimes there isn't."
Change the ending of the story to show
how the child would feel if no owl had
come. Write a new ending for the story,
and share it with your classmates.

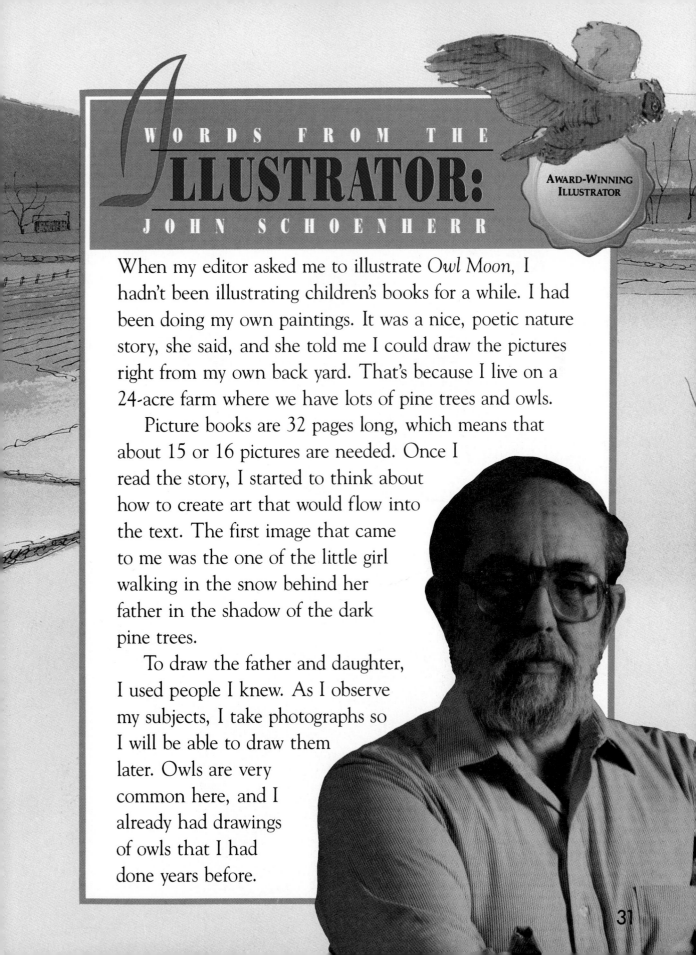

AWARD-WINNING ILLUSTRATOR

When my editor asked me to illustrate *Owl Moon*, I hadn't been illustrating children's books for a while. I had been doing my own paintings. It was a nice, poetic nature story, she said, and she told me I could draw the pictures right from my own back yard. That's because I live on a 24-acre farm where we have lots of pine trees and owls.

Picture books are 32 pages long, which means that about 15 or 16 pictures are needed. Once I read the story, I started to think about how to create art that would flow into the text. The first image that came to me was the one of the little girl walking in the snow behind her father in the shadow of the dark pine trees.

To draw the father and daughter, I used people I knew. As I observe my subjects, I take photographs so I will be able to draw them later. Owls are very common here, and I already had drawings of owls that I had done years before.

Crinkleroot's
BOOK OF
ANIMAL TRACKING

JiM ARNOSKY

AWARD-WINNING
AUTHOR AND
ILLUSTRATOR

Crinkleroot's Book of

ANIMAL TRACKING

written and illustrated by

JIM ARNOSKY

Hello. You've been following Crinkleroot tracks. My name is Crinkleroot, and these are my tracks.

I can hear a fox turn in the forest, and spot a mole hole on a mountain. I can find an owl in the daytime.

When I walk about the forest, I leave signs that tell I've been around—my footprints. Animals leave marks and tracks that show where they have been and what they have been doing.

I can show you how I find signs of animals that live near me; then you can find signs of animals that live near you. One of the best places to look is around water.

Animals are attracted to streams and ponds, park fountains, and even damp patches of grass. There they find water to drink and food to eat.

This pond was created by beavers. Can you see the beaver signs?

Beavers have sharp teeth and can gnaw down a tree! Chewed-down trees and gnawed-off twigs are good beaver signs to look for.

Beavers create a pond by damming up a stream, using branches, sticks, and mud. A dam like this is a sure sign that beavers are living in the pond.

When a beaver fells a tree that is too heavy to drag to the water, it chews the tree into small logs and rolls each one into the pond. The beaver then pushes the floating log to wherever it is needed. Sometimes a beaver gets lucky, and the tree falls right into the pond.

Beavers use logs and chewed-off branches to build their homes, or lodges.

LODGE

ENTRANCE

MUDDY BOTTOM

FLOW

BEAVER

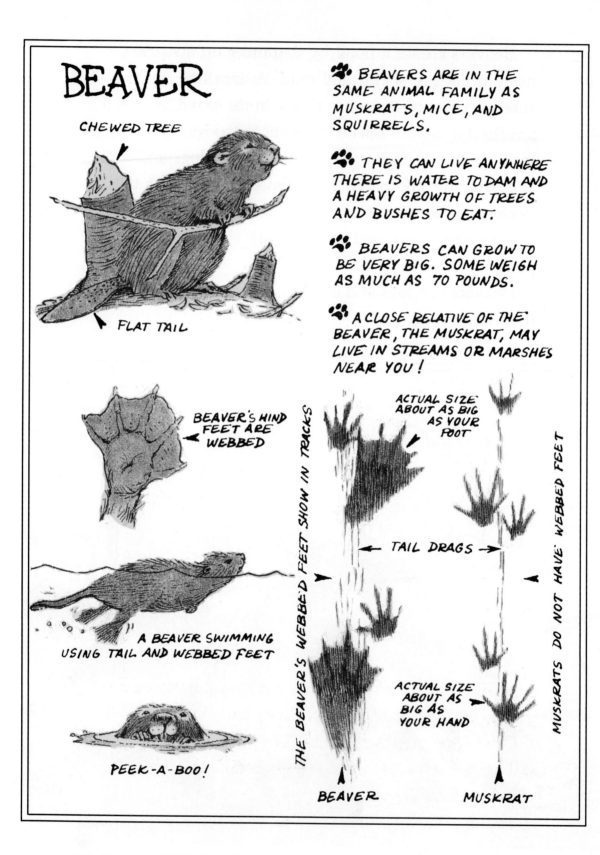

CHEWED TREE

FLAT TAIL

🐾 BEAVERS ARE IN THE SAME ANIMAL FAMILY AS MUSKRATS, MICE, AND SQUIRRELS.

🐾 THEY CAN LIVE ANYWHERE THERE IS WATER TO DAM AND A HEAVY GROWTH OF TREES AND BUSHES TO EAT.

🐾 BEAVERS CAN GROW TO BE VERY BIG. SOME WEIGH AS MUCH AS 70 POUNDS.

🐾 A CLOSE RELATIVE OF THE BEAVER, THE MUSKRAT, MAY LIVE IN STREAMS OR MARSHES NEAR YOU!

BEAVER'S HIND FEET ARE WEBBED

A BEAVER SWIMMING USING TAIL AND WEBBED FEET

PEEK-A-BOO!

THE BEAVER'S WEBBED FEET SHOW IN TRACKS

ACTUAL SIZE ABOUT AS BIG AS YOUR FOOT

TAIL DRAGS

ACTUAL SIZE ABOUT AS BIG AS YOUR HAND

MUSKRATS DO NOT HAVE WEBBED FEET

BEAVER   MUSKRAT

Beavers also eat the wood from trees they gnaw down. In autumn they gnaw off the small branches and store them on the bottom of the pond. In winter when the pond is frozen over, they will use these branches for food.

Let's wade around the shallow edges of the pond and look for other wildlife signs.

Here are webbed footprints, but these aren't beaver tracks. These tracks were made by an otter.

Otters are carefree critters. They play for hours, sliding down muddy spots on the pond bank and splashing into the water.

You may have seen otters sliding at the zoo.

OTTER

🐾 OTTERS ARE IN THE WEASEL FAMILY. SO ARE MINKS, BADGERS, AND SKUNKS. (AND WEASELS!)

🐾 OTTERS CAN GROW TO BE 20 POUNDS OR MORE.

🐾 IF YOU LIVE NEAR A RIVER, YOU MAY HAVE AN OTTER LIVING NEAR YOU!

🐾 IF YOU LIVE NEAR A WOODLOT, LOOK FOR SOME OF OTTER'S WEASEL RELATIVES.

WEBBED HIND FEET

OTTER TRACKS SHOWING WEBBED FEET

ACTUAL SIZE IS 3 INCHES

TAIL DRAG

TRACKS OF AN OTTER RUNNING

OTTERS ARE THE ONLY WEASELS MORE AT HOME IN WATER THAN ON LAND.

These footprints look like the prints of tiny human hands and feet. They were made by raccoons.

Raccoons eat anything they can catch or find. They even raid garbage cans. They come to the water to hunt for crayfish, frogs, snails, and freshwater clams.

Like many wild animals, raccoons are nocturnal. That means they are more active at night than during the day.

One night I watched a raccoon reach under the rocks in the shallow water of the pond. It was feeling for a crayfish hiding there.

The raccoon looked like a bandit in the moonlight.

RACCOON

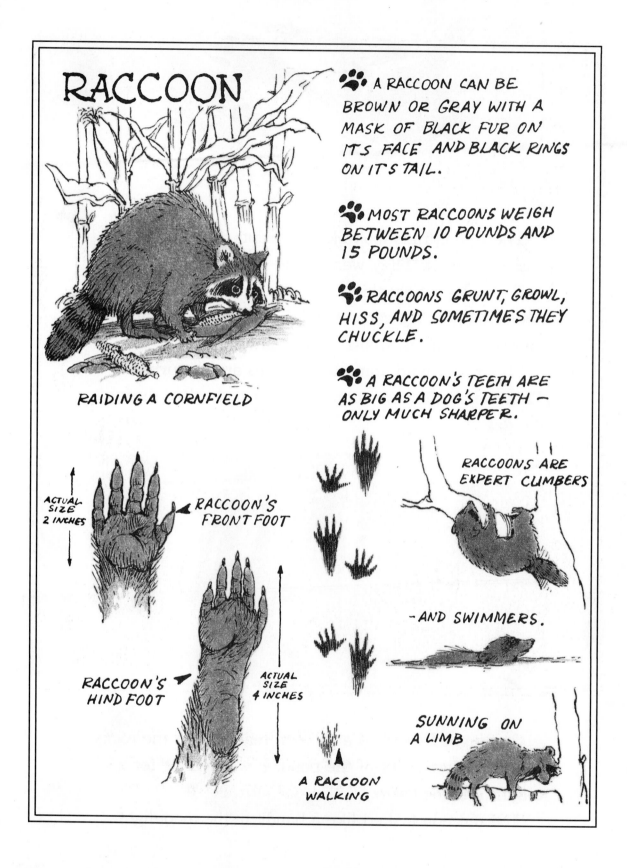

RAIDING A CORNFIELD

🐾 A RACCOON CAN BE BROWN OR GRAY WITH A MASK OF BLACK FUR ON ITS FACE AND BLACK RINGS ON ITS TAIL.

🐾 MOST RACCOONS WEIGH BETWEEN 10 POUNDS AND 15 POUNDS.

🐾 RACCOONS GRUNT, GROWL, HISS, AND SOMETIMES THEY CHUCKLE.

🐾 A RACCOON'S TEETH ARE AS BIG AS A DOG'S TEETH — ONLY MUCH SHARPER.

ACTUAL SIZE 2 INCHES

RACCOON'S FRONT FOOT

RACCOON'S HIND FOOT

ACTUAL SIZE 4 INCHES

A RACCOON WALKING

RACCOONS ARE EXPERT CLIMBERS

—AND SWIMMERS.

SUNNING ON A LIMB

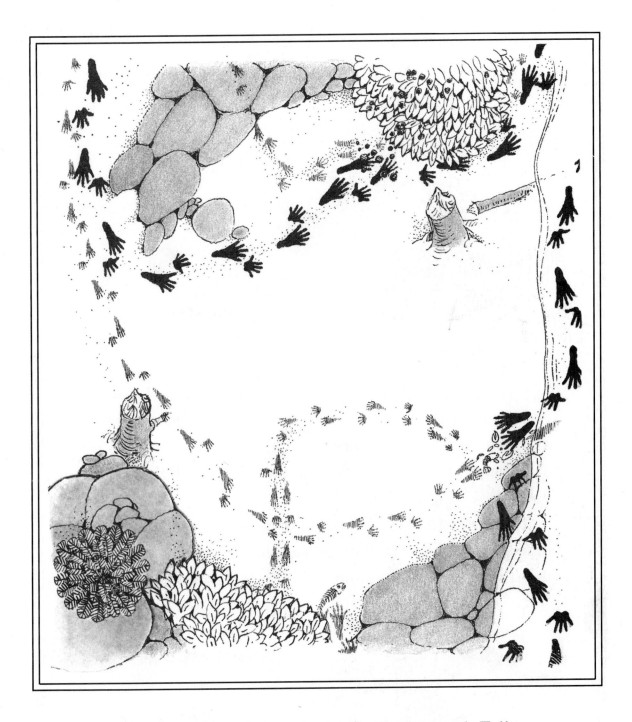

Here are lots of raccoon tracks in the mud. Follow them and see what they tell you. What did the big raccoons catch and eat? How many smaller raccoons were there?

Owls hunt at night. But I like to hunt for owls in the daytime. So can you. Here's how.

When an owl eats a mouse, it swallows it whole—tail and all.

The owl's stomach digests everything except the mouse bones and fur. The bones and fur form a ball that the owl coughs up and out onto the ground.

These balls of bones and fur are called owl pellets.
They collect on the ground around trees where owls
have been roosting. You can look for these pellets
around the trees near your home. If you find some, look
in the tree above for an owl sleeping the day away.
That's how I find owls in the daytime.

Here are some owl pellets. Can you see an owl in this
tree?

I've seen a lot of tracks here in the forest. I've even tracked fleas through the fur on a bear's back. But I can't seem to recognize these tracks next to my own.

Why, they must be yours.

Wherever you live, there are animals living near you. Look for the signs animals leave in parks and woodlots, on pavements and sidewalks, under trees, around streams and ponds, and in the snow. I can't promise you'll find any flea tracks, but you'll find something. And if you hear a soft swish in the night, go back to sleep. It's just a fox turning around somewhere in the forest.

Would you like to go animal tracking with Crinkleroot? Explain why or why not.

How does knowing about animal signs help you learn about animals?

How are nocturnal animals different from other animals?

Which animal would be the easiest to track? Which would be the most difficult? Why do you think so?

WRITE What animal signs can you look for where you live? Make a list.

A Day When Frogs Wear Shoes

from *MORE STORIES JULIAN TELLS*

by Ann Cameron • illustrated by Ann Strugnell

My little brother, Huey, my best friend, Gloria, and I were sitting on our front steps. It was one of those hot summer days when everything stands still. We didn't know what to do. We were watching the grass grow. It didn't grow fast.

"You know something?" Gloria said. "This is a slow day."

"It's so slow the dogs don't bark," Huey said.

"It's so slow the flies don't fly," Gloria said.

"It's so slow the ice cream wouldn't melt," I said.

"If we had any ice cream," Huey said.

"But we don't," Gloria said.

We watched the grass some more.

"We better do something," I said.

"Like what?" Gloria asked.

"We could go visit Dad," Huey said.

"That's a *terrible* idea," I said.

"Why?" Huey asked. "I like visiting Dad."

My father has a shop about a mile from our house, where he fixes cars. Usually it is fun to visit him. If he has customers, he always introduces us as if we were important guests. If he doesn't have company, sometimes he lets us ride in the cars he puts up on the lift. Sometimes he buys us treats.

"Huey," I said, "usually, visiting Dad is a good idea. Today, it's a dangerous idea."

"Why?" Gloria said.

"Because we're bored," I said. "My dad hates it when people are bored. He says the world is so interesting nobody should ever be bored."

"I see," Gloria said, as if she didn't.

"So we'll go see him," Huey said, "and we just won't tell him we're bored. We're bored, but we won't tell him."

"Just so you remember that!" I said.

"Oh, I'll remember," Huey said.

Huey was wearing his angel look. When he has that look, you know he'll never remember anything.

Huey and I put on sweat bands. Gloria put on dark glasses. We started out.

The sun shined up at us from the sidewalks. Even the shadows on the street were hot as blankets.

Huey picked up a stick and scratched it along the sidewalk. "Oh, we're bored," he muttered. "Bored, bored, bored, bored, bored!"

"Huey!" I yelled. I wasn't bored anymore. I was nervous.

Finally we reached a sign:

RALPH'S CAR HOSPITAL
Punctures
Rust
Dents & Bashes
Bad Brakes
Bad Breaks
Unusual Complaints

That's my dad's sign. My dad is Ralph.

The parking lot had three cars in it. Dad was inside the shop, lifting the hood of another car. He didn't have any customers with him, so we didn't get to shake hands and feel like visiting mayors or congressmen.

"Hi, Dad," I said.

"Hi!" my dad said.

"We're—" Huey said.

I didn't trust Huey. I stepped on his foot.

"We're on a hike," I said.

"Well, nice of you to stop by," my father said. "If you want, you can stay awhile and help me."

"O.K.," we said.

So Huey sorted nuts and bolts. Gloria shined fenders with a rag. I held a new windshield wiper while my dad put it on a car window.

"Nice work, Huey and Julian and Gloria!" my dad said when we were done.

And then he sent us to the store across the street to buy paper cups and ice cubes and a can of frozen lemonade.

We mixed the lemonade in the shop. Then we sat out under the one tree by the side of the driveway and drank all of it.

"Good lemonade!" my father said. "So what are you kids going to do now?"

"Oh, hike!" I said.

"You know," my father answered, "I'm surprised at you kids picking a hot day like today for a hike. The ground is so hot. On a day like this, frogs wear shoes!"

"They do?" Huey said.

"Especially if they go hiking," my father said. "Of course, a lot of frogs, on a day like this, would stay home. So I wonder why you kids are hiking."

Sometimes my father notices too much. Then he gets yellow lights shining in his eyes, asking you to tell the whole truth. That's when I know to look at my feet.

"Oh," I said, "we *like* hiking."

But Gloria didn't know any better. She looked into my father's eyes. "Really," she said, "this wasn't a real hike. We came to see you."

"Oh, I see!" my father said, looking pleased.

"Because we were bored," Huey said.

My father jumped up so fast he tipped over his lemonade cup. "BORED!" my father yelled. "You were BORED?"

He picked up his cup and waved it in the air.

"And you think *I* don't get BORED?" my father roared, sprinkling out a few last drops of lemonade from his cup. "You think I don't get bored fixing cars when it's hot enough that frogs wear shoes?"

"'This is such an interesting world that nobody should ever be bored.' That's what you said," I reminded him.

"Last week," Huey added.

"Ummm," my father said. He got quiet.

He rubbed his hand over his mouth, the way he does when he's thinking.

"Why, of course," my father said, "I remember that. And it's the perfect, absolute truth. People absolutely SHOULD NOT get bored! However—" He paused. "It just happens that, sometimes, they do."

My father rubbed a line in the dirt with his shoe. He was thinking so hard I could see his thoughts standing by the tree and sitting on all the fenders of the cars.

"You know, if you three would kindly help me some more, I could leave a half hour early, and we could drive down by the river."

"We'll help," I said.

"Yes, and then we can look for frogs!" Huey said. So we stayed. We learned how to make a signal light blink. And afterward, on the way to the river, my dad bought us all ice cream cones. The ice cream did melt. Huey's melted all down the front of his shirt. It took him ten paper napkins and the river to clean up.

After Huey's shirt was clean, we took our shoes and socks off and went wading.

We looked for special rocks under the water—the ones that are beautiful until you take them out of the water, when they get dry and not so bright.

We found skipping stones and tried to see who could get the most skips from a stone.

We saw a school of minnows going as fast as they could to get away from us.

But we didn't see any frogs.

"If you want to see frogs," my father said, "you'll have to walk down the bank a ways and look hard."

So we decided to do that.

"Fine!" my father said. "But I'll stay here. I think I'm ready for a little nap."

"Naps are boring!" we said.

"Sometimes it's nice to be bored," my father said.

We left him with his eyes closed, sitting under a tree.

Huey saw the first frog. He almost stepped on it. It jumped into the water, and we ran after it.

Huey caught it and picked it up, and then I saw another one. I grabbed it.

It was slippery and strong and its body was cold, just like it wasn't the middle of summer. Then Gloria caught one too. The frogs wriggled in our hands, and we felt their hearts beating. Huey looked at their funny webbed feet.

"Their feet are good for swimming," he said, "but Dad is wrong. They don't wear shoes!"

"No way," Gloria said. "They sure don't wear shoes."

"Let's go tell him," I said.

We threw our frogs back into the river. They made little trails swimming away from us. And then we went back to my father.

He was sitting under the tree with his eyes shut. It looked like he hadn't moved an inch.

"We found frogs," Huey said, "and we've got news for you. They don't wear shoes!"

My father's eyes opened. "They don't?" he said.

"Well, I can't be right about everything. Dry your feet. Put your shoes on. It's time to go."

We all sat down to put on our shoes.

I pulled out a sock and put it on.

I stuck my foot into my shoe. My foot wouldn't go in.

I picked up the shoe and looked inside.

"Oh no!" I yelled.

There were two little eyes inside my shoe, looking out at me. Huey and Gloria grabbed their socks. All our shoes had frogs in them, every one.

"What did I tell you," my father said.

"You were right," we said. "It's a day when frogs wear shoes!"

Julian's father says the world is so interesting that nobody should ever be bored. Do you agree? Why or why not?

Is Julian correct when he says that visiting Dad is a dangerous idea? Tell why you think as you do.

What does Dad mean when he says that frogs wear shoes?

WRITE   Imagine you spent a hot summer day near a river. Write a letter to a friend telling about what you did.

ANIMAL FACT/
ANIMAL FABLE

by Seymour Simon • illustrated by Manuel Garcia

Many of us like to watch animals. You may have a pet dog or cat. At times you may notice that your pet moves its tail differently when it's happy than when it's angry. After watching your pet for a long time, you can probably tell a great deal about what each kind of tail movement means.

But even if you watch animals closely, it is sometimes easy to mistake what is happening. For example, a bat flutters around in an odd way in the night sky. Some people may think that bats are blind and can't see where they are going.

If bats are really blind, that belief is true; it is a fact. But suppose the bat flies in that odd way for another reason, and is not really blind. Then the belief is a fable; it is not true.

On the following pages, we'll look at some common beliefs about animals. Guess if each belief is a fact or a fable; then turn the page to find the answer. You will also discover why scientists think the belief is a fact or a fable.

AWARD-WINNING
AUTHOR

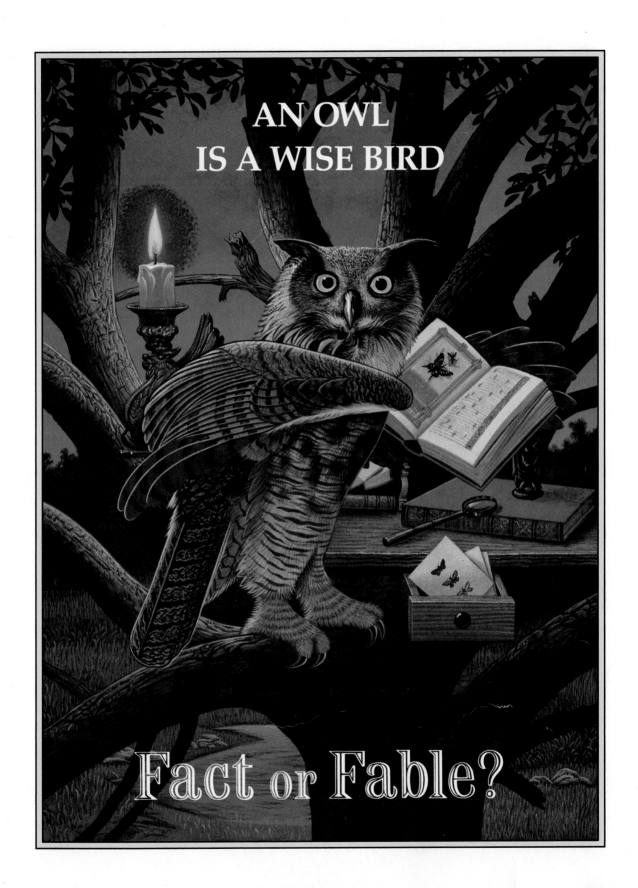

AN OWL
IS A WISE BIRD

Fact or Fable?

Fable

Some people think an owl looks wise because of its wide-open eyes. But for a bird its size, the owl has a tiny brain. If you say a person is as wise as an owl, you are saying he or she is a birdbrain!

An owl moves its whole head when it looks around. It never moves its eyes from side to side. Its eyes are very sharp. It can see even small objects, such as mice, that are very far away.

THE ARCHER FISH
SHOOTS DOWN ITS FOOD

Fact or Fable?

Fact

The archer fish shoots down insects that live near the banks of streams and ponds. When an archer sees an insect, it swims toward it. The archer raises its mouth close to the surface of the water. Then it squirts a spray of water.

The water drops hit the insect and the insect falls into the water. One swift gulp and the insect becomes a meal for the finned sharpshooter.

RACCOONS
WASH THEIR FOOD

Fact or Fable?

Fable

Raccoons sometimes dip their food into water before they eat, but they are not washing it. A raccoon's throat is not very large. It has trouble swallowing large pieces of food. Dipping food in water makes it softer and easier to swallow. When a raccoon finds a mushy piece of fruit, he doesn't wash it no matter how dirty it is. He just gulps it down right away.

What is the most interesting animal fact you learned? Explain your answer.

How are the animals in the selection alike, and how are they different?

WRITE Choose an animal and write your own fact or fable about it. Then write a paragraph explaining the fact or correcting the fable. Share it with your classmates.

Following Animal Friends

You have read about many different animals. Which animals would you like to learn more about? Give reasons for your choices.

WRITER'S WORKSHOP

Choose an animal you might like to follow and watch. Where would you go to look for the animal? What special things would you need? Write a paragraph telling step by step what you would do. Read your paragraph to your classmates.

Writer's Choice: You might want to write about watching something else, such as plants as they change with the seasons. Decide what you will write about and how you will share your work.

THEME

Flights of Fancy

Have you ever wanted to soar like an eagle? The next story and poem will take you on a trip. In the story, you'll travel with an armadillo and an eagle high above the Earth. As you read the poem, you will wish you had wings of your own.

CONTENTS

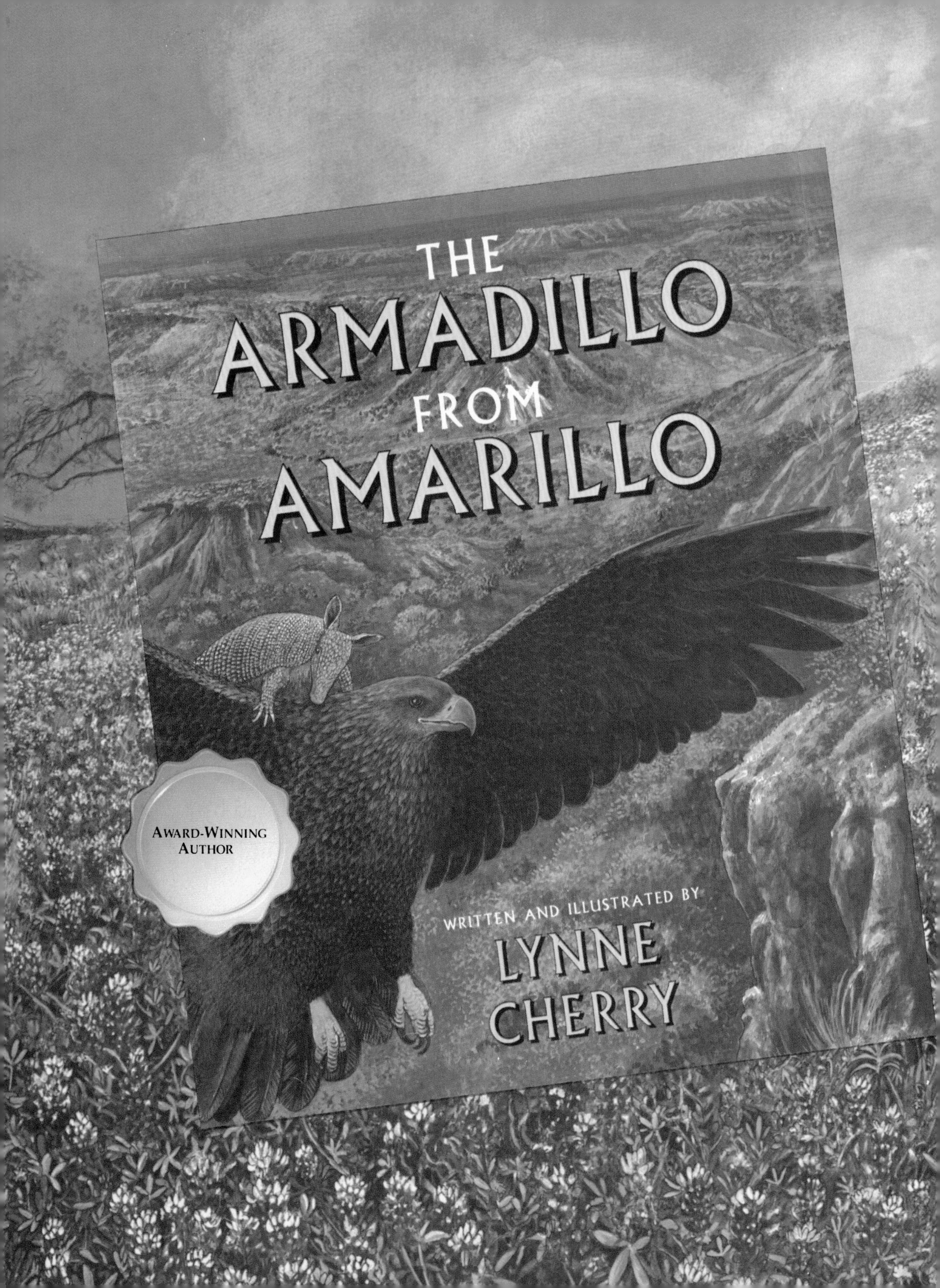

THE
ARMADILLO
FROM
AMARILLO

AWARD-WINNING
AUTHOR

WRITTEN AND ILLUSTRATED BY
LYNNE
CHERRY

AN ARMADILLO from Texas wondered, "Where in the world am I?
What's out beyond these tangled woods? What's out beyond the sky?"
So Armadillo packed up his things and left his home behind.
He headed off on a northeast course to seek what he could find.

Dear Brillo,
Hi and warm regards from your cousin Sasparillo. I lay my head and slept today on a blue bluebonnet pillow.
Love,
Sasparillo

BRILLO ARMADILLO
PHILADELPHIA ZOO
CHILDREN'S ZOO
3400 W. GIRARD AVE.
PHILADELPHIA
PA 19104

He traveled to the nearby city
of San Antonio,
and from the top of the highest tower,
he saw where he might go.

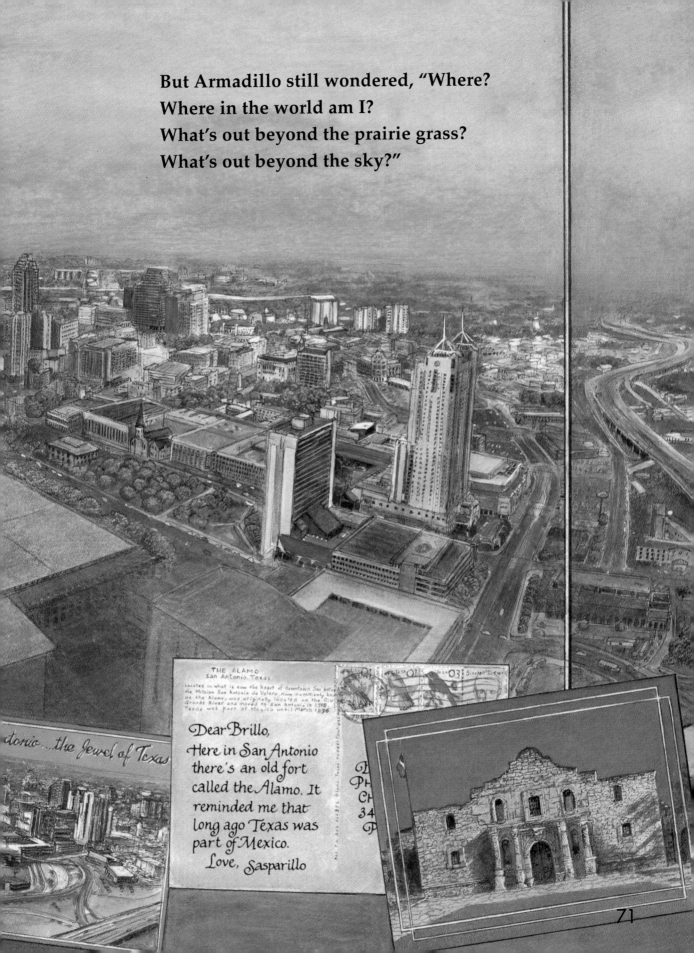

But Armadillo still wondered, "Where?
Where in the world am I?
What's out beyond the prairie grass?
What's out beyond the sky?"

Dear Brillo,
Here in San Antonio
there's an old fort
called the Alamo. It
reminded me that
long ago Texas was
part of Mexico.
Love, Sasparillo

THE ALAMO
San Antonio, Texas

71

He followed the river past twisted oaks,
through ancient juniper trees
shared by warblers and vireos
and Carolina chickadees.

The landscape changed dramatically
through woodland, towns, and plains.

ENCHANTED ROCK
AUSTIN, TEXAS

Armadillo explored canyons
and walked through heavy rains.

He walked for weeks and came to Austin,
continued west and north
to Abilene and Lubbock,
he hiked and sallied forth.

Dear Brillo,
I much prefer the
night to traveling
during the day. So
sometimes I look for
a cranny or nook to
sleep the sun away.
Love, Sasparillo

POST CAR
BRILLO ARMA
PHILADELPH
CHILDREN'S
3400 W. GIRAR
PHILADELPHIA, PA

73

Armadillo often along the way
climbed up to higher ground.
He scurried up the canyon walls
and stopped to look around.

Howdy from Texas!

Dear Brillo,
I'm near Amarillo.
This land is cool and
flat! It's definitely
an inadequate
Armadillo habitat!
I'll be the only
Armadillo who lives
near the city of
Amarillo!
Sasparillo

POST CARD

20 JUNE
1993

BRILLO ARMADILLO
PHILADELPHIA ZOO
CHILDREN'S ZOO
3400 W. GIRARD AVE.
PHILADELPHIA, PA
19104

How different were the plains above—
flowers went on for a mile!
Armadillo decided to settle down
and stay there for a while.

But Armadillo still wondered, "Where,
where in the world *am* I?
Perhaps I'd have a better idea
if I could somehow fly."

One day he asked the golden eagle,
as she came breezing by,
"What can I do for a bird's-eye view
from up in the big blue sky?"

"Hop on my back," said the eagle.
"I'll fly you wide and far.
And then you'll see, eventually,
where in the world we are."

Upward and upward the eagle flew.
Armadillo held on tight.
"With my tail-tip curled I'll explore the world
from morning until night!"

Palo Duro
Canyon
Amarillo,
TEXAS

PALO DURO CANYON
Near Amarillo and Canyon Texas
The Lighthouse—The Best Known Formation
in Palo Duro Canyon State Park

Dear Brillo,
Except for the canyons like
this one here, this land is
flat, flat, flat! And
an Armadillo near
Amarillo should wear
a scarf and hat!
Love,
Sasparillo

POST CARD

BRILLO ARMADILLO
PHILADELPHIA ZOO
CHILDREN'S ZOO
3400 W. GIRARD AVE.
PHILADELPHIA, PA
19104

Armadillo looked down below and asked,
"Where in the world *are* we?"
"We're over a prairie, and in the distance,
that's Amarillo you see.

"We've flown over the prairie.
We've flown over a town.
Amarillo means yellow, my dear little fellow,
and the prairie's all yellow and brown!"

"I see Amarillo," said Armadillo.
"Could we see all Texas, though?
And if we fly *higher* up into the sky,
could we see New Mexico?

"Or if we fly *higher* up into the sky,
could we see the entire earth?"
"Well, certainly, surely, if you hold on securely,
we'll try!" cried the eagle with mirth.

"*Amarillo's* a *city*?" asked Armadillo.
To this the eagle replied,
"Yes, Amarillo's a city in *Texas*,
the *state* where we reside.

"And Texas is in the *United States*,
our *country* wide and dear,
on the *North American continent*,
which is on the *earth*, a sphere.

"This sphere is called a *planet*,
of nine we are just one,
and as we converse, in the *universe*,
these planets turn round the sun."

81

Armadillo held tightly to Eagle's neck,
afraid of a long, long fall.
From over his shoulder, with the air getting colder,
this is what he saw.

They flew so high up into the sky
that Texas they saw below—
the part they call the Panhandle—
and the state of New Mexico.

"With my tail-tip curled I'll explore the world!"
Armadillo said to his friend.
Through the clouds they twirled, in the wind
they whirled, and up they were hurled again!

And when they looked up they could see into space.
They'd flown up into thin air.
"It's hard to breathe here! I'd like to leave here!
Eagle, homeward let's repair!"

"We're very high now," said Eagle,
"on the edge of air and space.
The atmosphere's ending, we should be descending,
but what a remarkable place!"

"There must be a way to fly higher up,
bringing some air aboard.
Perhaps we should travel to Cape Canaveral,"
Eagle said as she soared.

As they spoke of Cape Canaveral—
the rocket-launching place—
a shuttle took off with a roar of fire
and headed out toward space.

Eagle had a brilliant thought
and whistled a happy tune.
"Let's hitch a trip on this rocket ship
and fly up to the moon!"

With a burst of speed the eagle flew
in the path of the rocket ship.
It took Armadillo and her aboard
and continued on its trip.

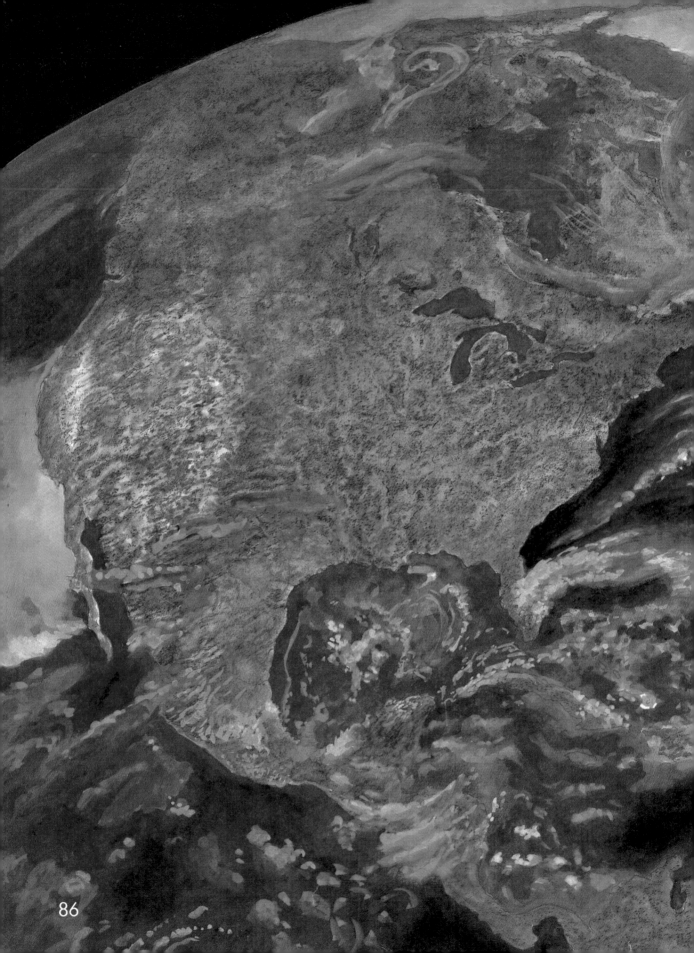

The higher they flew, the farther they saw—
Louisiana and Arkansas!
And there were some other countries below—
they could see Cuba and Mexico!

The spaceship then zoomed so high up
that Armadillo could not tell
where a country began or ended,
or where its borders fell.

The earth was now so far away—
so very, very far.
"I'm wondering," said Armadillo,
"where in the world we are."

"We're *out* of this world," said the eagle
to the armadillo, her friend.
"Ten miles from earth starts the universe
right at the atmosphere's end."

From space the earth was a big round ball,
with swirling clouds of white
against a deep-blue background,
like the blue-black sky at night.

Planets shone around them,
reflecting starlike light.
In that silent room floating in the dark,
they traveled through the night.

Before them was earth's silver moon—
a white and glowing sphere.
They hovered there, floating in thin air,
over craters, with no fear.

And as they watched in wonder,
the earth rose on the horizon.
They sat and gazed at their far-off home—
watched earth-set and earth-risin'.

Armadillo said, "I'm homesick.
Hey, Eagle, let's go back.
Let's go back down to our yellow town,
away from this blue and black."

The rocket began a downward arc,
then flew over land and sea.
The adventurous pair flew through the air
to their home by the yellow prairie.

He'd wondered where in the world he was,
and now Armadillo knew.
He said, "I know where, in the scheme of things,
I am, Eagle, thanks to you!

"I now live near Amarillo,
a city that's rather small,
which is in the state of Texas,
one of fifty states in all,

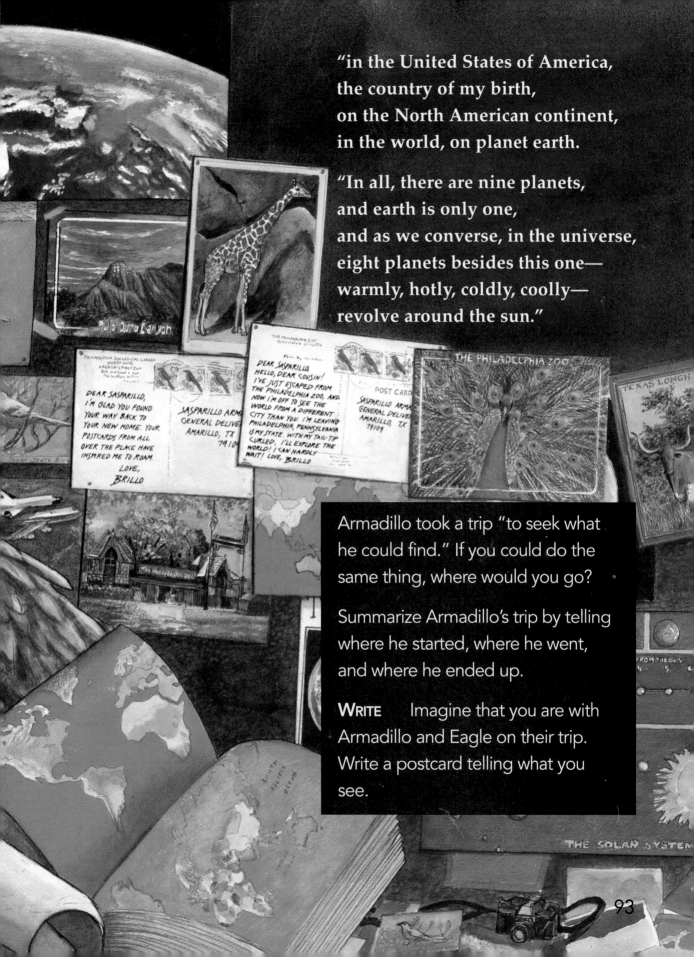

"in the United States of America,
the country of my birth,
on the North American continent,
in the world, on planet earth.

"In all, there are nine planets,
and earth is only one,
and as we converse, in the universe,
eight planets besides this one—
warmly, hotly, coldly, coolly—
revolve around the sun."

Armadillo took a trip "to seek what he could find." If you could do the same thing, where would you go?

Summarize Armadillo's trip by telling where he started, where he went, and where he ended up.

WRITE Imagine that you are with Armadillo and Eagle on their trip. Write a postcard telling what you see.

I AM FLYING!

by Jack Prelutsky • illustrated by Ken Bowser

I am flying! I am flying!
I am riding on the breeze,
I am soaring over meadows,
I am sailing over seas,
I ascend above the cities
Where the people, small as ants,
Cannot sense the keen precision
Of my aerobatic dance.

I am flying! I am flying!
I am climbing unconfined,
I am swifter than the falcon,
And I leave the wind behind,
I am swooping, I am swirling
In a jubilant display,
I am brilliant as a comet
Blazing through the Milky Way.

I am flying! I am flying!
I am higher than the moon,
Still, I think I'd best be landing,
And it cannot be too soon,
For some nasty information
Has lit up my little brain—
I am flying! I am flying!
But I fly without a plane.

94

Flights of Fancy

Both the armadillo and the person in the poem took journeys. How are Armadillo's trip and the trip in the poem different? Which one did you like better? Tell why.

WRITER'S WORKSHOP

Think about how Earth looked to Armadillo when he was walking from place to place. Then think about how it looked when he was riding on Eagle's back. Write a paragraph telling how Earth looks when you are on the ground and how it looks from the air. Tell what is the same or what is different.

Writer's Choice:
You might want to write about two other things that are different from each other. Your topics might be two sports or two kinds of music. Plan what you will write, and carry out your plan.

T H E M E

Unusual Pets

Have you ever had an unusual pet? Do you think it might be fun to have one? The selections that follow are about a kind of animal that is not usually someone's pet.

C O N T E N T S

THE SECRET OF THE SEAL

by Deborah Davis • illustrated by Judy Labrasca

Kyo's uncle George has come to visit, seeking a seal for a city zoo. Kyo[1] has a hard time keeping his uncle away from the spot on the bay where his secret friend is hidden under the ice.

Kyo couldn't fall asleep that night. When he heard deep snores from his uncle's bedroll on the floor across the room, Kyo slipped out of bed, went to the window, and parted the curtains.

The world outside was lit by an eerie silver glow. A big round disc of a moon hung in the sky. The snoring stopped, and Kyo heard rustling from George's bed. Turning, he saw the moonlight shining on his uncle's face.

Kyo quickly closed the curtains. The snoring resumed, and he put on his clothes as soundlessly as he could. Then he pulled on his boots and parka, eased the door open just enough for him to squeeze through, and found himself out in the nighttime glow.

He set out directly for Tooky's hole in the ice. Halfway there he remembered that if she had not been using the hole, it would have closed up, and he had not brought the pick. Still, he hurried on to their meeting place.

The hole was blocked by new ice, just as Kyo had expected. His throat tightened when he saw the frozen barrier. Sitting on the edge of the hole, he brought his heel down as hard as he could, but it bounced off the surface.

---

[1] Kyo [kē'·ō]

He leaned back, raising both feet high, and tried to smash the ice again. It didn't even crack. He considered jumping on the ice to break it open, but he knew that if he succeeded he'd likely drown.

"I'm not a seal," he said aloud. His words sounded small and lost in the strange night air. He lay on his belly and rubbed the surface of the ice with his mitten like he would wipe steam off his mother's mirror, hoping for a view of his friend below the surface.

"I don't know if you can hear me, Tooky," he said to the ice blocking his way, "but I'm doing my best to keep my uncle away from you. Keep checking this hole, Tooky, and when you see it open you'll know it's safe to come up and visit with me again. I don't know how long it will be, and I hope you don't give up. Please keep checking. I miss you!"

Kyo jumped up and started running back to his house. He stopped shortly, though, and ran back to the hole.

"I love you!" he called to his friend, and headed for the house again. As he ran the world darkened. He looked up to see the moon disappear behind a blanket of clouds. Snowflakes fell all around him. He slowed his pace as it got harder to see the path through the flurrying snow.

As Kyo reached his small dark house, the air cleared and the brightness returned. He turned to look out at the ice. Millions of freshly fallen flakes sparkled in the moonlight. Suddenly very sleepy, Kyo slipped inside the warm house and got into bed.

Smack smack! Thwack THWACK! Kyo opened his eyes hoping to see Tooky clapping her flippers, but instead he saw his mother making bread by the stove. He quickly glanced over at his uncle's sleeping place on the floor and sat up with a start when he saw it was empty.

"Mama, where's my uncle?" Kyo asked worriedly. Annawee[2] answered without turning from her dough.

"He's off seal hunting. He tried to wake you, but you slept as soundly as a baby. You can follow him after you eat. He didn't take his snowmobile, and he left good tracks in the snow that fell last night."

Tracks! Kyo thought. *I* left tracks last night! He'll see them.

Kyo jumped out of bed and pulled on his clothes.

"Can I take my breakfast with me, Mama? I want to go help my uncle. I don't want to miss anything." He made his eyes as big as he could, but he didn't have to worry about convincing her.

"I'm glad you want to help him. It's rare that we get to see Ahko.[3]" She wrapped generous portions of breakfast in a clean towel, which Kyo stuffed into his parka.

---

[2] Annawee [ă′·nă·wē]

[3] Ahko [ă′·kō]

"Goodbye!"

He ran out the door with his parka half open, pulling his mittens on his hands. He saw the tracks immediately: two sets of boots, big ones over little ones, following the path to Tooky's hole.

Kyo started to run down the path but changed his mind, going to the snowmobile instead. He jumped on the seat and sat for a moment, trying to remember how to start the engine. He turned the key, and the machine wheezed, coughed, and was silent. He tried again, and this time the whole thing shook and sputtered and growled—then was still. Kyo swung off the seat and kicked one of the runners.

"You have to start!" he shouted at the hulk of metal. Glancing at the house, Kyo saw Annawee's face appear briefly in the window. Before she reached the door Kyo was back on the snowmobile seat, turning the key. This time he remembered to turn the throttle.

The engine burst into its loud growl. Annawee's shouts were lost in the snowmobile roar as Kyo turned the throttle more and the machine lurched forward, pulling the sledge and cage away from the house and toward the great ice.

The world flew by. Thrilled by the speed, Kyo forgot for a moment that there was any danger, either to himself or to his friend at the end of the path. Rounding a protruding slab of ice, Kyo felt the machine lift slightly off one runner. Scared that he might tip over, he slowed down a little.

George came into view. He was thrusting a pick into Tooky's old breathing hole to reopen it. Stunned by George's action and feeling helpless to stop him, Kyo let the snowmobile slide to a halt.

George finished hacking at the ice and looked up. He waved to Kyo, stepped back from the reopened hole, and picked up his rifle. Kyo jumped down and ran toward George, hoping that Tooky would not appear.

Just then her round head popped up in the hole.

"Don't come up!" Kyo tried to yell, but the words caught in his throat. Tooky slid onto the ice and began her awkward lope toward the boy.

"No!" he cried, and she stopped, confused. George lifted his gun and the movement caught the seal's eye. She whirled and bobbed quickly toward the hole.

George fired, dropped the gun, and raced toward the seal, who continued toward her escape, slowing as she reached it. George dove onto the ice and grabbed her tail just as her head dipped into the water.

"Kyo!" he yelled. "Come and help me pull her out! She'll die if she falls in."

Kyo reached them just seconds later. Together he and his uncle heaved and pulled the heavy, limp animal safely onto the ice.

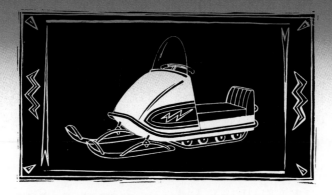

Kyo sank down beside the still form.

"Whew! That was close!" panted George. He too sat down beside the seal.

"She looks dead."

"Oh, no, Kyo. Remember, I told you that the darts only put the seal to sleep for a few hours. She hasn't been hurt at all."

Kyo wiped his eyes and nose on his sleeve. George glanced at the snowmobile and back to Kyo.

"You sure surprised me when you came flying down here on my machine. But then I could tell you were a smart boy. You learned quickly how to drive it."

Kyo was silent. He stared down at Tooky, wishing she would jump up and dive into the water before anyone could stop her.

"I'm not angry that you drove the snowmobile out here, Kyo. That was quick thinking. I'm just glad you didn't get hurt. You knew I'd find a seal here, didn't you? Or is there another boy with boots your size who walks out here often, sometimes with only the moon to light his way?"

Kyo ignored his uncle, who stood up and went to retrieve the gun. Kyo put his ear against Tooky and listened for her heartbeat. It was strong and even. Then he put his ear to her nose and felt her warm breath.

Satisfied that the seal was alive, Kyo sat up, his thoughts racing. He was afraid to tell his uncle that Tooky was a friend. George would never believe him. He would laugh at him or, worse, tell his parents and they would all have a good laugh at him during supper that night.

"Animals have a hard life," George had told him the day before. "They have to fight and struggle to survive." Maybe Tooky would be better off in the zoo after all, Kyo thought. Maybe she'd like having fish handed to her every day. Maybe fish are hard to find on her own. He wished he could just ask her, but he knew that even awake she could not answer him.

George drove the snowmobile up close to the seal, parking the cage beside her. "Give me a hand with her—say, Kyo, how did you know this seal was a female?"

"I've seen her before," Kyo said quietly. "And I won't help you put her in your rotten cage!" Kyo turned and ran off, away from his uncle and the sleeping seal and the settlement.

Shaking his head, George gently maneuvered the heavy seal into the cage. Then he started the engine and drove carefully back to the house.

Kyo walked in a wide circle that took him far out on the ice, then inland to the base of the mountains. He found a sunny spot out of the wind and sat down, took out his knife and stone, and began to carve.

Near dusk he stood up, stretched his legs, and started to climb. Stopping partway up the slope to catch his breath, he turned and faced the valley below. He picked out his own house among the others, all dark against the graying terrain. The snowmobile was parked near the house and George's figure moved beside it.

A shadow passed over Kyo, and he looked up to see a great snowy owl glide over his head. The huge bird's outspread wings beat slowly and firmly against the evening air.

Suddenly it dropped to the snow, talons first, then quickly lifted off with a small, white ball of fur wriggling in its grasp. The owl had caught its prey. It would eat that night.

Kyo realized he was hungry, too. Hours ago he'd consumed the food his mother had packed for him. He started down the mountainside.

A loud clamor of barking dogs greeted Kyo as he approached his home. He saw Tooky lying still in the cage. He hung his fingers on the wire and leaned his face against it.

George came out of the house just as Kyo turned to go inside. He mumbled a greeting to his uncle and brushed by him.

Annawee sat in her favorite chair, a kerosene lamp glowing on either side of her, needle in hand, cloth heaped in her lap. Kudlah[4] sat bent over a snowshoe frame, weaving narrow strips of leather, pulling them taut and securing them to the frame. They both looked up as Kyo came in and watched him slowly remove his parka.

"You look troubled, Kyo," said his father.

"I'm sad," he said, nodding. "And hungry."

Kudlah put down the snowshoe and went to the stove, where he ladled steaming soup into a bowl and set it on the table for the tired boy. He sat at the table with Kyo and watched him pour spoonfuls of soup into his mouth without pause. When the bowl was empty, Kyo asked for more. "Just half a bowl, please." Kudlah filled it and sat down again. When that was gone, too, Kyo pushed away the bowl and looked at his father.

---

[4] Kudlah [kŏŏd′·lă]

"I saw a big white owl on the mountainside catch a mouse for its supper and I didn't feel sad. I was happy for the owl because it flew so smoothly and had no other way to get food." He stopped, but Kudlah just waited. Annawee had set down her needle. Her hands lay still in her lap.

"My uncle was happy to catch the seal today, but I'm not pleased for him at all. He says she'll be happier when someone gives her fish every day, but I wonder if she doesn't like to swim fast and catch her own."

No one spoke, and no one laughed.

"I've never seen a seal swim under water, but they sure are clumsy on land. They're really made to swim, aren't they? I bet they're graceful in the sea, like this!" Kyo picked up his spoon and made it swoop through the air.

"Whoosh . . . whoosh . . . whoosh!"

The door opened and George walked in, head hanging. Kudlah filled another bowl with soup and set it on the table for his brother-in-law. "Come eat, George. You must be hungry. Are you ready for the long trip back to the city tomorrow?"

George washed his hands and sat down heavily beside Kyo. "I am ready," he replied. "But the seal is not. She should have awakened by now. Something went wrong. She is dead."

Kyo jumped up and ran outside without stopping to put on his parka. The others stayed seated.

His heart pounding, Kyo unfastened the door to the cage and crawled inside, moving carefully around his friend. He bent to feel her breath on his ear. Nothing. He listened for a heartbeat and heard it, a little sluggish but steady.

Then he lifted his head again for a breath. It seemed like forever before he felt a gentle tickle against his skin. He waited, stock still, until he felt it again.

Sighing with relief, Kyo leaned back, stroking Tooky's head.

"Why won't you wake up?" He spoke to her still form. "I don't know how to help you, but first I want to get you out of this cage."

Kyo crawled out and stalked into the house.

"She isn't dead," he announced to the waiting adults, who looked surprised.

"Kyo," George said gently, "I know you're upset about this. But she isn't breathing—"

"She is, too!" Kyo interrupted. "You just have to be patient. You don't understand seals! Sometimes they don't breathe when they sleep. But she *will* wake up!" His voice shook, a little unsure, but he rushed on. "You have to help me move her. She will feel better when she's near the water."

"You have seen this animal before, Kyo?" asked Kudlah.

Kyo nodded his head.

"And she lets you get so close that you can watch how she breathes?"

"Yes," Kyo spoke quietly.

Kudlah wrinkled his brow pensively, then stood up.

"If the seal is dead, George, she'll be of no use to us. Her meat will be spoiled by the drug in your darts, and we must throw her back in the bay.

"And if she is alive"—he looked at Kyo—"perhaps the boy can wake her up."

Kudlah put on his parka and boots and left the house.

Annawee put aside her sewing and also got ready to go outside. George sat with his elbows on the table, head in his hands.

"Ahko!" Annawee spoke sharply to her brother. "Let us do what Kudlah says." George got up slowly and followed the others outside.

In the light of the rising moon the seal did indeed look dead. "We're going to help you now, Tooky," Kyo whispered through the wire.

As George climbed on the snowmobile, Kyo said to his father, "I want to move her with the dog team."

"All right," agreed Kudlah.

With four of them working, the sledge was unharnessed from the snowmobile and hitched up to the dogs in no time. Kudlah handed the traces to his son.

"You know how to do this, Kyo. George, here is your chance for a dogsled ride."

Eagerly Kyo stepped up onto the sledge. George got on, too, and sat down. Commanding the restless dogs to run, Kyo guided the sledge away from the house. He let the dogs go as fast as they wanted, and he looked back often to check on the seal. When the hole was in sight, Kyo slowed the team and brought the sledge to a halt.

"I have to unhitch the dogs so Tooky won't be scared when she wakes up," Kyo said to his uncle. He jumped down and began to free the sledge.

"The seal—what do you call her, Tooky?—won't wake up, Kyo. I'm afraid that the sleeping medicine was too strong for her." Kyo either didn't hear his uncle or ignored him. He unhitched the dogs from the sledge but kept them harnessed together.

"Here," Kyo said, holding out the traces to his uncle. "I need your help. Take the dogs to the house. Please."

Reluctantly George did as the boy asked. He led the dogs away from the sledge but stopped when he'd gone about fifty yards.

Kyo climbed back into the cage. Cradling the seal's head in his lap, he sang a song his mother used to sing to him.

Wake up, sleepyhead,
Wake up, dreaming one.
The sky is shining now—
Come outside and see the sun!

Three times Kyo sang the verse. On the fourth, Tooky opened her eyes and picked up her head. Kyo nudged her gently toward the cage door. The seal wriggled her body backward through the opening.

Seeing the animal leave the cage, the dogs and George rushed forward to prevent her escape. Kyo looked up to see the yapping dogs approaching and commanded them to halt. The dogs obeyed, and George stopped behind them.

On the ice now, Tooky sniffed in different directions as if to get her bearings. Kyo scrambled out of the cage, clapped his mittens together, and laughed. Then he dashed ahead, and Tooky skittered along behind him. George started after them again, but this time he stopped himself and watched them go.

When they reached Tooky's hole in the ice, Kyo sat by the edge and faced the seal. She put her nose close to his and gently brushed it with her whiskers.

Leaning back, Kyo broke the thin layer of newly formed ice easily with the heel of his boot. He stood up and watched Tooky dive into the sea. Then he turned from the hole to follow his uncle, who was already walking back to the house, dog traces in hand, leaving the empty cage behind.

Kyo treats Tooky like a pet. Would you act the same way? Why or why not?

Do you think Kyo is ever lonely? Explain your answer.

What are some of the reasons why Kyo doesn't tell anyone about Tooky?

WRITE Why do you think Kyo chose the song he sang to Tooky? Write a song of your own that you think Tooky might like.

Seal

by William J. Smith
illustrated by Arnold Lobel

See how he dives
From the rocks with a zoom!
See how he darts
Through his watery room
Past crabs and eels
And green seaweed,
Past fluffs of sandy
Minnow feed!
See how he swims
With a swerve and a twist,
A flip of the flipper,
A flick of the wrist!
Quicksilver-quick,
Softer than spray,
Down he plunges
And sweeps away;
Before you can think,
Before you can utter
Words like "Dill pickle"
Or "Apple butter,"
Back up he swims
Past Sting Ray and Shark,
Out with a zoom,
A whoop, a bark;
Before you can say
Whatever you wish,
He plops at your side
With a mouthful of fish!

Unusual Pets

Think about what you learned in "The Secret of the Seal" and the poem "Seal." Do you think a seal is an unusual pet for an Inuit boy? Explain your answer.

WRITER'S WORKSHOP

Imagine that you have read about someone trying to capture a wild animal. How would you feel? Write a persuasive paragraph for a newspaper, telling what you think. Give your most important reasons last.

Writer's Choice:

You might want to give your opinion about something else. It could be something that happened in the classroom or in your community. Write a paragraph telling what happened and why you feel as you do. Share it with your classmates.

CONNECTIONS

Multicultural Connection

Inuit Sculpture

Many Canadian Eskimos, or *Inuits* (which means "the first people"), create beautiful soapstone sculptures. These carvings are made from a soft, heavy, grayish stone. They reveal much about Inuit culture and about the animals that live in the northern Canadian wilderness.

Inuit carvings often show the traditional way of life, such as ice fishing or hunting. They also show seals, walruses, and other Arctic animals in lifelike poses.

Work with a group to have a **First People Art Festival.** Using clay, create your own version of Inuit sculpture, showing at least two animals. Then display your work for classmates to see and touch. You may want to create your own legend or tale to tell about the piece.

Soapstone sculpture is an important source of income for many Canadian Eskimos. Carvings made of the soft, heavy stone have become popular in the United States and Canada.

Science Connection

Arctic Animals

Make a list of the animals you sculpted for the First People Art Festival. Write down facts you already know about the animals. Then find new information from other sources. Share your information with classmates.

Art Connection

Creature Feature

Make a colorful poster about one of the Arctic animals. Include drawings or pictures of the animal and its home. Display your poster on a wall or bulletin board.

Unit Two

Puzzlers

Listen, I know a secret!
Will you share your secrets with me?
N. M. Bodecker

People have always been puzzled by things they cannot understand. They sometimes write tales to explain what may have happened. An African folktale tells how a long drought was finally ended. But no one has explained what caused the people of the ancient Mayan cities to disappear. Finding solutions to such puzzles is not always easy, but the selections in this unit prove that it is often possible.

THEMES

BOOKSHELF

RAINY RAINY SATURDAY
by Jack Prelutsky
All of us have felt cooped up on a rainy Saturday.
This collection of poems will bring a little sunshine
into a rainy day.
Award-Winning Author
Harcourt Brace Library Book

THE MAGIC FAN
written and illustrated by Keith Baker
Yoshi uses an unusual fan to help him solve the
problems in his village. This beautiful book has
magic of its own within the pages.
Award-Winning Author
Harcourt Brace Library Book

PETER AND THE WOLF

retold and illustrated by Michèle Lemieux

This is the classic tale of Peter and his friends—
a bird, a cat, and a duck—and their encounter
with a hungry wolf.

Award-Winning Illustrator

THE SLY SPY

by Marjorie and Mitchell Sharmat

Olivia Sharp, Agent for Secrets, is solving cases again.
This time, Olivia is the one with the problem. Another
agent is spoiling her business, and she wants
him stopped.

Award-Winning Authors

SEBASTIAN (SUPER SLEUTH) AND THE CRUMMY YUMMIES CAPER

by Mary Blount Christian

Sebastian, the world's greatest canine detective and
a master of disguise, must try to solve the case of
Crummy Yummies. This case will require Sebastian's
most difficult disguise—that of an ordinary dog!

Award-Winning Author

T H E M E

Whether the Weather

Sometimes the weather can be a puzzle. It is not always an easy puzzle to solve. The selections that follow focus on puzzles and problems involving weather and nature.

C O N T E N T S

125

BRINGING THE RAIN TO KAPITI PLAIN

by Verna Aardema / pictures by Beatriz Vidal

This is the great
    Kapiti Plain,
All fresh and green
    from the African rains—
A sea of grass for the
    ground birds to nest in,
And patches of shade for
    wild creatures to rest in;
With acacia trees for
    giraffes to browse on,
And grass for the herdsmen
    to pasture their cows on.

But one year the rains
    were so very belated,
That all of the big wild
    creatures migrated.
Then Ki-pat helped to end
    that terrible drought—
And this story tells
    how it all came about!

127

This is the cloud,
   all heavy with rain,
That shadowed the ground
   on Kapiti Plain.

This is the grass,
    all brown and dead,
That needed the rain
    from the cloud overhead—
The big, black cloud,
    all heavy with rain,
That shadowed the ground
    on Kapiti Plain.

These are the cows,
    all hungry and dry,
Who mooed for the rain
    to fall from the sky;

To green-up the grass,
    all brown and dead,
That needed the rain
    from the cloud overhead—
The big, black cloud,
    all heavy with rain,
That shadowed the ground
    on Kapiti Plain.

This is Ki-pat,
    who watched his herd
As he stood on one leg,
    like the big stork bird;
Ki-pat, whose cows
    were so hungry and dry,
They mooed for the rain
    to fall from the sky;

To green-up the grass,
    all brown and dead,
That needed the rain
    from the cloud overhead—
The big, black cloud,
    all heavy with rain,
That shadowed the ground
    on Kapiti Plain.

This is the eagle
   who dropped a feather,
A feather that helped
   to change the weather.
It fell near Ki-pat,
   who watched his herd
As he stood on one leg,
   like the big stork bird;
Ki-pat, whose cows
   were so hungry and dry,
They mooed for the rain
   to fall from the sky;

To green-up the grass,
   all brown and dead,
That needed the rain
   from the cloud overhead—
The big, black cloud,
   all heavy with rain,
That shadowed the ground
   on Kapiti Plain.

This is the arrow
   Ki-pat put together,
With a slender stick
   and an eagle feather;
From the eagle who happened
   to drop a feather,
A feather that helped
   to change the weather.
It fell near Ki-pat,
   who watched his herd
As he stood on one leg,
   like the big stork bird;

Ki-pat, whose cows
   were so hungry and dry,
They mooed for the rain
   to fall from the sky;
To green-up the grass,
   all brown and dead,
That needed the rain
   from the cloud overhead—
The big, black cloud,
   all heavy with rain,
That shadowed the ground
   on Kapiti Plain.

This is the bow,
    so long and strong,
And strung with a string,
    a leather thong;
A bow for the arrow
    Ki-pat put together,
With a slender stick
    and an eagle feather;
From the eagle who happened
    to drop a feather,
A feather that helped
    to change the weather.

It fell near Ki-pat,
    who watched his herd
As he stood on one leg,
    like the big stork bird;
Ki-pat, whose cows
    were so hungry and dry,
They mooed for the rain
    to fall from the sky;
To green-up the grass,
    all brown and dead,
That needed the rain
    from the cloud overhead—
The big, black cloud,
    all heavy with rain,
That shadowed the ground
    on Kapiti Plain.

This was the shot
    that pierced the cloud
And loosed the rain
    with thunder LOUD!
A shot from the bow,
    so long and strong,
And strung with a string,
    a leather thong;
A bow for the arrow
    Ki-pat put together,
With a slender stick
    and an eagle feather;
From the eagle who happened
    to drop a feather,
A feather that helped
    to change the weather.

It fell near Ki-pat,
    who watched his herd
As he stood on one leg,
    like the big stork bird;
Ki-pat, whose cows
    were so hungry and dry,
They mooed for the rain
    to fall from the sky;
To green-up the grass,
    all brown and dead,
That needed the rain
    from the cloud overhead—
The big, black cloud,
    all heavy with rain,
That shadowed the ground
    on Kapiti Plain.

So the grass grew green,
   and the cattle fat!
And Ki-pat got a wife
   and a little Ki-pat—

Who tends the cows now,
   and shoots down the rain,
When black clouds shadow
   Kapiti Plain.

How do you think it feels to be in a drought?

How does Kapiti Plain change during the drought?

Summarize the causes that lead to the rain that ends the drought.

WRITE Ki-pat feels that he has to do something to end the drought. Write a paragraph about something you or someone you know had to do in order to solve a problem.

RAIN SIZES

by John Ciardi

Rain comes in various sizes.
Some rain is as small as a mist.
It tickles your face with surprises,
And tingles as if you'd been kissed.

Some rain is the size of a sprinkle
And doesn't put out all the sun.
You can see the drops sparkle and twinkle,
And a rainbow comes out when it's done.

Some rain is as big as a nickel
And comes with a crash and a hiss.
It comes down too heavy to tickle.
It's more like a splash than a kiss.

When it rains the right size and you're wrapped in
Your rainclothes, it's fun out of doors.
But run home before you get trapped in
The big rain that rattles and roars.

APRIL RAIN SONG

by Langston Hughes

AWARD-WINNING
AUTHOR

Let the rain kiss you.
Let the rain beat upon your head with silver liquid drops.
Let the rain sing you a lullaby.

The rain makes still pools on the sidewalk.
The rain makes running pools in the gutter.
The rain plays a little sleep-song on our roof at night—

And I love the rain.

RAINY RAINY SATURDAY

by Jack Prelutsky

AWARD-WINNING
AUTHOR

It's Saturday
and what a pain,
no school today
but lots of rain,

and Mother tells me
when it pours,
"The weather's bad
so stay indoors."

I'd rather go
out in the yard,
but no! it's raining
much too hard,

so I will stay
inside and play
this rainy
rainy Saturday.

FLAMES AND REBIRTH

AWARD-WINNING AUTHOR

from *YELLOWSTONE FIRES:*
Flames and Rebirth
by Dorothy Hinshaw Patent
photos by William Muñoz
and Others

SETTING THE STAGE

In the summer of 1988, fires in Yellowstone National Park made news across the nation. Headlines screamed that the park had burned up, that nothing was left. Luckily, those stories weren't true. Yellowstone is alive and well. Much of the park did burn, but nature has been rebuilding. What really happened that summer? Why in Yellowstone? And what can we expect for the future of the park?

Background:
Smoke from the fires often blocked out the sun.

Forests for Burning

Yellowstone will heal because it is used to fire. In our lives, we normally think in terms of a few years or at most a human lifetime. But the cycles of nature often are longer than that. In 1988, Yellowstone hadn't had huge fires since the early 1700s, although some large ones burned in the 1800s. The forests were ready to burn again.

Eighty percent of the park's trees are lodgepole pines—miles and miles of them. Lodgepoles grow quickly. But they don't live very long compared to some other trees. After about two hundred years, the trees in a lodgepole forest begin to die. The dead and dying trees are blown down in storms. As more and more trees fall, young ones grow up to take their place, and the floor of the forest keeps collecting wood from fallen trees.

In areas where lots of rain falls, the dead wood on the forest floor is attacked by fungus and bacteria which break it down. But in dry forests, like those of Yellowstone, most of the dead trees stay where they fall. Just like in a fireplace, this wood acts as fuel for fire. A lodgepole forest that is three hundred years old has so much dead wood that walking through it is difficult. There are logs to climb over everywhere.

Rain and Drought

Normally, the Yellowstone area gets most of its moisture in the wintertime from snow. When spring

grow. In normal years, some rain also comes to Yellowstone in June, July, and August.

It took hundreds of years to set the stage for the 1988 fires. Much of the forest grew for over two hundred years without really big fires, and the dead wood built up on the forest floor. Then, for six years in the 1980s, snowfall was light during the winter, making drought conditions build.

In April and May of 1988, much more than the normal amount of rain fell. This helped the small trees and other plants between the mature forest trees grow well. When June came, the park managers were not worried. They had no reason to suspect that June would only have 20 percent of its normal rainfall and that almost no rain would fall in early July. They didn't know that 1988 would turn out to be the driest summer ever recorded since the park was established 116 years

SHOULD WE PUT OUT FIRES?

Until 1972, all fires that started in national parks and that could be reached were fought. People saw fires as bad. After all, they killed trees and made ugly scars on the land. But as scientists learned more and more about nature, they realized that fire has its place. They learned that when dry northern forests go too long without fire, more and more nutrients are locked up in the dead and living trees. There aren't enough nutrients available for the trees to grow and stay healthy. It's as if the forests were starving.

Fire–A Part of Nature

When Yellowstone was founded over a hundred years ago, there were more open meadows than there are today. The lodgepole forests have been taking over the open land, leaving less room for grazing animals like elk to feed. Fires help maintain meadows by burning the small trees growing along their edges.

A Change of Policy

Once scientists understood that fire is an important natural force with healthy effects, they decided that not all fires should be fought after all. In 1972, a new policy began. If a fire was started by lightning in a national forest or a national park, it wasn't put out unless it caused a threat to private property

managers felt this new policy would help keep the parks
and forests more natural.

Above:
The 1988 fires helped open up
meadows in which elk could graze.

Background:
Lightning strikes cause many fires,
but most burn out quickly.

YELLOWSTONE AFLAME

A number of fires started in Yellowstone and in the surrounding forests during June of 1988. The park itself lies at the center of a region called the "Yellowstone Ecosystem," or "Greater Yellowstone Area." Besides Yellowstone, the ecosystem includes Grand Teton National Park and the lands of several national forests. No one can hunt, cut trees for wood, or mine in a national park. But in the forests, these activities can take place.

Lightning sparked a fire on June 14 in the Storm Creek area of Custer National Forest north of the park. Officials decided to let it burn, since it was far from towns, homesites, or ranches. No one thought this fire would become destructive. But as the summer went on, it became one of the most dangerous of all, growing to more than 95,000 acres.

Left:
The fire approaches Old Faithful.

Background:
The North Fork Fire burns just a few miles south of Mammoth Hot Springs on September 10, the same day Mammoth was evacuated.

Fires started in the park itself as well. Many were allowed to burn, and most went out quickly by themselves before covering an acre. But by July 15, things began to look bad. The expected rainfall hadn't arrived, and the forests were very dry. About 8,000 acres in the park had burned. And winds were making the fires grow dangerously fast.

Trying to Stop the Fires

Less than a week later, on July 21, park officials decided to fight all fires in the park. By then, almost 17,000 acres had already burned. The next day, a cigarette left by a careless wood gatherer started a fire in the North Fork area of the Targhee National Forest just west of the park. Fire fighters began to fight it the same day. Meanwhile, in the northeast part of the park, two fires that started the second week in July joined to become the Clover-Mist Fire.

Unfortunately, the wind whipped up on July 23, two days after the decision to fight all fires. The combination of the wind and the dry conditions was too much for the fire fighters. The North Fork Fire, less than 30 acres when reported, grew to 500 acres before it was a day old, despite the fact that smoke jumpers—parachuting fire fighters—were sent in right away. The wind also carried bits of burning material such as pine cones, called "firebrands," as far as a half mile in front of the fire. Officials didn't know it at the time, but the uncontrolled burning of Yellowstone had begun.

FIGHTING THE FIRES

As the fires burned, they threatened more than just Yellowstone's forests. The Clover-Mist and Storm Creek fires both came within a few miles of Cooke City and Silver Gate, Montana, two communities near the northeast corner of the park. Luckily, fire fighters

148

stopped them from consuming the towns. The North Fork Fire threatened Canyon Village, inside the park. On August 24, five hundred tourists and employees were evacuated as the fire came within five miles of the area.

Uncontrollable Burning

The Yellowstone fires were awesome. No matter how hard they tried, humans could not stop them. The raging winds helped the flames race across the landscape. When firebrands hit dry timber, entire trees burst into flames. The trees were dry, and lots of dead wood lay on the forest floor. Trees killed by bark beetles stood in some areas, perfect fuel for flames. The rain didn't fall, and the trees were tinder-dry. These conditions are perfect for fires to crown. When that happens, the flames consume the entire tree. The tops, or crowns, of even the living trees become engulfed in flame. These are called "canopy fires," since they burn the branches that form a covering, or canopy, over the forest. Canopy fires are especially difficult to fight. The heat from the intense fire increases the wind, and the wind carries firebrands as far as two miles to unburned areas, starting still more fires.

Canopy fires can move very quickly, frustrating efforts to stop them. And firebrands can start fires behind the fire fighters, making their work especially dangerous. They could become quickly surrounded by flames and trapped.

Background: The canopy fires of 1988 were an awesome sight.

Above:
A burned marsh in fall 1988.

Background:
Meadows as well as forests burned in 1988.

AFTERMATH

Snow and rain stopped the worst of the fires in September. But here and there, fires smoldered and occasionally flamed up until November. By the time it was all over, eight huge fires had covered almost half of the park. The northwestern corner was hardest hit. But the southeast and northeast corners were also badly burned. Altogether, eleven major fires had burned in the Greater Yellowstone Area, fought by 9,500 fire fighters. In the wake of the fires, officials decided temporarily to fight all fires in national parks and forests until a new policy that coordinated fire management plans in parks and the surrounding national forests could be worked out.

How Much Burned?

Now it was time to see how much damage the fires had really caused. Television and newspaper stories made it sound as if Yellowstone was destroyed. But it wasn't. Many of the fires had not crowned and become canopy fires. They had just burned along the forest floor and not killed the trees. Other fires had burned over meadows and sagebrush.

Park researchers looked at the soil to see if plant roots and seeds had been killed. Fortunately, even in the worst burn areas, the roots of bushes were still alive below the ground. Lodgepole cones opened by the fire had scattered seeds all over the forest floor. They would grow to form the new forest.

Fire and Wildlife

Many people worried about the park animals during the fires. Would they be burned? It is difficult to count animals killed in fires, especially small ones. But the bodies of fewer than three hundred large animals, mostly elk, were found out of the thousands that roam the park. When the fire approached, bison, elk, deer, and pronghorn just moved away. Throughout the park, animals grazed near the fires. They were more disturbed by the noisy helicopters that flew overhead than by the flames.

Right:
Animals like the coyote benefited from the fires.

Background:
Yellowstone bison like these will be healthier after eating the nutritious grass that follows fire.

Some birds benefited during the fires. They hunted for food near the edges of the fires, feeding on small animals that were escaping. Young bald eagles had already flown from their nests before the fires threatened them, so they escaped. One osprey nest was burned before the young could fly.

THE FUTURE

Signs of renewal were already clear in the spring of 1989. Twenty kinds of grasses sprouted on the burned forest floor, mixed with flowers such as delicate shooting stars. The burned meadows grew more vigorously than before, with a healthy, deep green glow, nourished by the nitrogen and other nutrients released by the fires. The new growth is not only healthy and green, it actually contains more nutrients for the animals like elk that eat it. Grazers prefer the grass and other plants in recently burned areas, and it makes them healthier than grass in unburned meadows.

The lodgepole pine seeds covering the forest floor also began to grow into new trees that year. They were tiny and difficult to see, but they were there. By the end of the growing season, they had reached an inch and a half in height. Between the new seedlings, the roots of bushes and shrubs had sent up new growth, giving the blackened forest some greenery.

As Time Goes On

Around 100 to 150 years after the forest has burned, the weak trees will begin to die and fall to the forest floor. The cycle will begin to turn back toward its beginning, with fuel for future fires starting to build up underneath the trees. And later on, probably sometime during the twenty-third century, the forests of Yellowstone will burn again.

What was the most interesting thing you learned from this selection?

Is it usually a good thing to let fires burn? Tell your reasons for thinking as you do.

Think about this saying: "You can't fool Mother Nature." Do you think this saying is a good one? Tell why or why not.

WRITE The park managers changed their policy about fighting all forest fires. Write a persuasive paragraph telling why you think that was a wise or an unwise decision.

Background and Above:
Fireweed thrives after fires or in disturbed areas, including along roadsides.

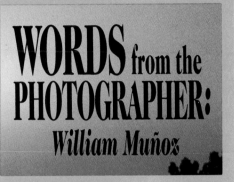

WORDS from the PHOTOGRAPHER:
William Muñoz

This photograph of William Muñoz feeding a baby camel shows his interest in wildlife.

In the summer of 1988, when the fires started, Dorothy Hinshaw Patent, the author of *Yellowstone Fires: Flames and Rebirth,* began talking to me about doing a book. In September, I went to Yellowstone Park and started taking pictures. The park was closed, but I got a permit to go in and take photographs of the fire damage. When I got the photos back, it was clear that we could return in the spring, and see the rebirth.

I take many, many pictures for a book like this. If there is a particular theme we want to bring out—in this case, it was the damage and the new growth—I try to find pictures that will show that. This was a very hot fire, and we wanted our readers to be able to see the bare, scorched earth that was left behind.

Living in Montana, I know the kind of destruction a forest fire can cause. In fact, I went to Yellowstone expecting to see things worse than they actually were. Radio, television, and newspapers sometimes make things sound worse than they are. What people don't always realize is that there are positive things about forest fires. Yellowstone was very overgrown. It needed to be cleaned out. There are areas that now have new growth in them, new grasses and wildflowers. Those areas will probably become a big meadow, which is very positive. Meadows support more wildlife than forests do.

Down by Lake Yellowstone, in a burn area, I recently saw a new osprey nest. This osprey would not have nested in the forest. Ospreys need an open area. In the next twenty years, if the number of ospreys increases in the park as a result of the fire, that's a positive thing.

Whether the Weather

Think about the problems and solutions you have read about. Would you have solved the problems differently? Why or why not?

Writer's Workshop

Poets often write about the weather. Write a poem about any type of unusual weather. You might write about a blizzard, a thunderstorm, a hurricane, or an ice storm.

Writer's Choice:
What do you think about weather now that you have read the selections? Choose and plan your own way to respond. Then carry out your plan.

THEME

Being Clever

How much difference is there between playing a trick and being clever? Careful thinking is needed for each one. As you read the selections that follow, you will see how being clever *and* tricky helps solve some problems but may create others.

CONTENTS

Lon Po Po

A RED-RIDING HOOD STORY FROM CHINA

ED YOUNG

Once, long ago, there was a woman who lived alone in the country with her three children, Shang, Tao, and Paotze. On the day of their grandmother's birthday, the good mother set off to see her, leaving the three children at home.

Before she left, she said, "Be good while I am away, my heart-loving children; I will not return tonight. Remember to close the door tight at sunset and latch it well."

But an old wolf lived nearby and saw the good mother leave. At dusk, disguised as an old woman, he came up to the house of the children and knocked on the door twice: bang, bang.

Shang, who was the eldest, said through the latched door, "Who is it?"

"My little jewels," said the wolf, "this is your grandmother, your Po Po."

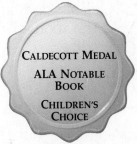

CALDECOTT MEDAL

ALA NOTABLE BOOK

CHILDREN'S CHOICE

"Po Po!" Shang said. "Our mother has gone to visit you!"

The wolf acted surprised. "To visit me? I have not met her along the way. She must have taken a different route."

"Po Po!" Shang said. "How is it that you come so late?"

The wolf answered, "The journey is long, my children, and the day is short."

Shang listened through the door. "Po Po," she said, "why is your voice so low?"

"Your grandmother has caught a cold, good children, and it is dark and windy out here. Quickly open up, and let your Po Po come in," the cunning wolf said.

Tao and Paotze could not wait. One unlatched the door and the other opened it. They shouted "Po Po, Po Po, come in!"

At the moment he entered the door, the wolf blew out the candle.

"Po Po," Shang asked, "why did you blow out the candle? The room is now dark."

The wolf did not answer.

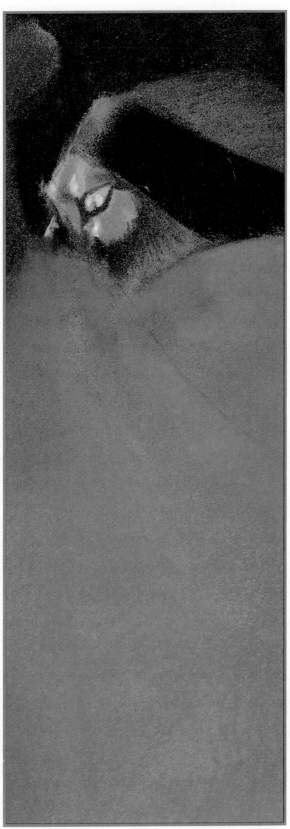

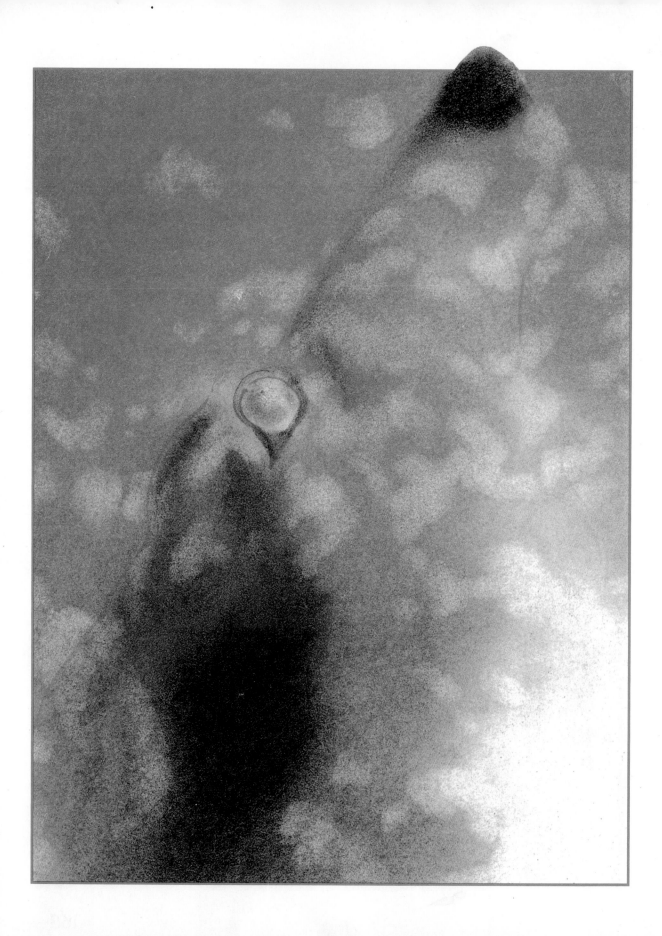

Tao and Paotze rushed to their Po Po and wished to be hugged. The old wolf held Tao. "Good child, you are so plump." He embraced Paotze. "Good child, you have grown to be so sweet."

Soon the old wolf pretended to be sleepy. He yawned. "All the chicks are in the coop," he said. "Po Po is sleepy too." When he climbed into the big bed, Paotze climbed in at one end with the wolf, and Shang and Tao climbed in at the other.

But when Shang stretched, she touched the wolf's tail. "Po Po, Po Po, your foot has a bush on it."

"Po Po has brought hemp strings to weave you a basket," the wolf said.

Shang touched grandmother's sharp claws. "Po Po, Po Po, your hand has thorns on it."

"Po Po has brought an awl to make shoes for you," the wolf said.

At once, Shang lit the light and the wolf blew it out again, but Shang had seen the wolf's hairy face.

"Po Po, Po Po," she said, for she was not only the eldest, she was the most clever, "you must be hungry. Have you eaten gingko nuts?"

"What is gingko?" the wolf asked.

"Gingko is soft and tender, like the skin of a baby. One taste and you will live forever," Shang said, "and the nuts grow on the top of the tree just outside the door."

The wolf gave a sigh. "Oh, dear. Po Po is old, her bones have become brittle. No longer can she climb trees."

"Good Po Po, we can pick some for you," Shang said.

The wolf was delighted.

Shang jumped out of bed and Tao and Paotze came with her to the gingko tree. There, Shang told her sisters about the wolf and all three climbed up the tall tree.

The wolf waited and waited. Plump Tao did not come back. Sweet Paotze did not come back. Shang did not come back, and no one brought any nuts from the gingko tree. At last the wolf shouted, "Where are you, children?"

"Po Po," Shang called out, "we are on the top of the tree eating gingko nuts."

"Good children," the wolf begged, "pluck some for me."

"But Po Po, gingko is magic only when it is plucked directly from the tree. You must come and pluck it from the tree yourself."

The wolf came outside and paced back and forth under the tree where he heard the three children eating the gingko nuts at the top. "Oh, Po Po, these nuts are so tasty! The skin so tender," Shang said. The wolf's mouth began to water for a taste.

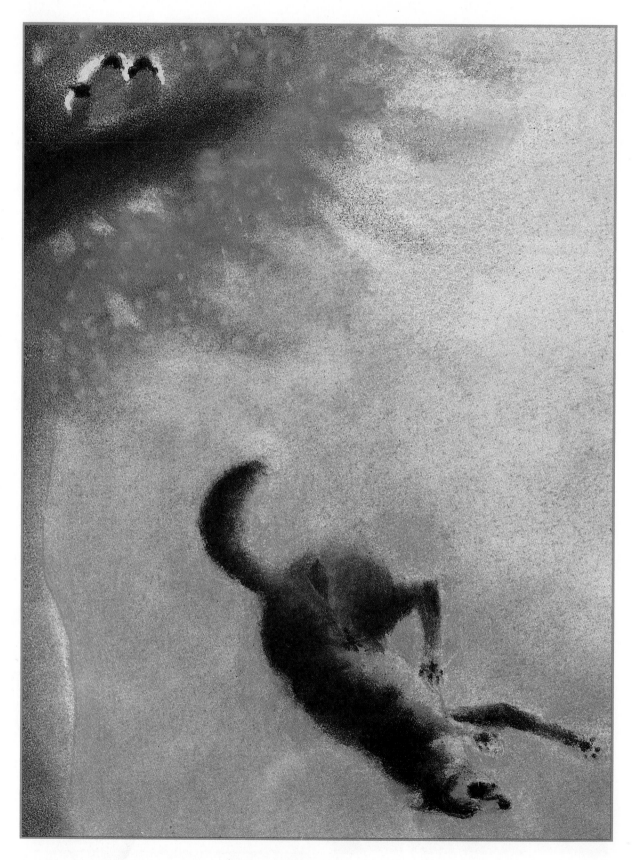

Finally, Shang, the eldest and most clever child, said, "Po Po, Po Po, I have a plan. At the door there is a big basket. Behind it is a rope. Tie the rope to the basket, sit in the basket and throw the other end to me. I can pull you up."

The wolf was overjoyed and fetched the basket and the rope, then threw one end of the rope to the top of the tree. Shang caught the rope and began to pull the basket up and up.

Halfway she let go of the rope, and the basket and the wolf fell to the ground.

"I am so small and weak, Po Po," Shang pretended. "I could not hold the rope alone."

"This time I will help," Tao said. "Let us do it again."

The wolf had only one thought in his mind: to taste a gingko nut. He climbed into the basket again. Now Shang and Tao pulled the rope on the basket together, higher and higher.

Again, they let go, and again the wolf tumbled down, down, and bumped his head.

The wolf was furious. He growled. "We could not hold the rope, Po Po," Shang said, "but only one gingko nut and you will be well again."

"I shall give a hand to my sisters this time," Paotze, the youngest, said. "This time we shall not fail."

Now the children pulled the rope with all of their strength. As they pulled they sang, "Hei yo, hei yo," and the basket rose straight up, higher than the first time, higher than the second time, higher and higher and higher until it nearly reached the top of the tree. When the wolf reached out, he could almost touch the highest branch.

But at that moment, Shang coughed and they all let go of the rope, and the basket fell down and down and down. Not only did the wolf bump his head, but he broke his heart to pieces.

"Po Po," Shang shouted, but there was no answer.

"Po Po," Tao shouted, but there was no answer.

"Po Po," Paotze shouted. There was still no answer. The children climbed to the branches just above the wolf and saw that he was truly dead. Then they climbed down, went into the house, closed the door, locked the door with the latch and fell peacefully asleep.

On the next day, their mother returned with baskets of food from their real Po Po, and the three sisters told her the story of the Po Po who had come.

Do you think the story is frightening? Why or why not?

How do the girls outsmart the wolf?

How do you think the girls' mother feels when she learns what happened?

WRITE   What are some ways that you can tell whether you can trust someone? Make a list.

WORDS ABOUT THE
AUTHOR
AND
ILLUSTRATOR:
ED YOUNG

Ed Young was born in China in 1931, the Chinese Year of the Sheep. There is a belief among the Chinese that people born in the Year of the Sheep are good at art. That belief is true of Ed Young.

Mr. Young grew up in Shanghai, one of China's biggest cities. People from all over the world live in Shanghai. Ed Young had friends from many races and cultures. He liked living with so many different kinds of people.

As a boy, Ed Young had a busy imagination. "I drew everything that happened to cross my mind," he remembers, "airplanes, people, a tall ship that my father was very proud of, a hunter and a bird dog that came out of my head—I have always been happiest doing my own thing."

When Mr. Young was twenty years old, he came to the United States. He soon decided to study art and to work for a magazine. "I knew no matter what I did in life, it would have to be first and foremost related to art," he says. After a few years, he began to illustrate children's books.

Making the illustrations for *Lon Po Po* took some special thinking. To make his drawings look real, Mr. Young had to learn how wolves communicate with their bodies. He also had to remember how the children in China lived and even how the trees grew. Ed Young feels that if he learns everything about the people and the places in a story, his drawings can help make them real to others.

When he is working on a book, Mr. Young starts with a tiny picture, about two inches square. He doesn't plan this picture. "It just comes out of my head," he says. Then he goes to the book editor to talk about ideas for the book. They also decide when the book must be finished. After that, Mr. Young reads about the place where the story happens and makes a set of pictures. "Then I can see what I don't know about the story," he says. He keeps studying until he finds what he needs to know. Finally, he decides on the best kind of pictures to illustrate the story. He may choose to make paper collages, water color paintings, or pencil drawings to match the mood of the story.

Mr. Young thinks the story and pictures need to work together to make a good book. "There are things that words can do that pictures never can," he says. He also thinks there are pictures that words can never describe. The story and pictures together should do what neither one can do alone.

THE CROW
AND
THE PITCHER

from *Belling the Cat and Other Aesop's Fables*

retold in verse by Tom Paxton

"I'm dying of thirst!" cawed the crow in despair.
He looked in a pitcher—some water was there!
He stuck in his beak for a drink, but—hello—
It seemed that the level of water was low.
His beak couldn't reach it,
His chances looked slim,
But then an idea came leaping at him.
He picked up a pebble, flew back in a flash;
It dropped in the pitcher and fell with a splash.
Again and again came the black-feathered flier.
Each pebble that fell brought the sweet water higher.
At last, when the water was near to the brink,
This quick-thinking bird took a well-deserved drink.
So wisdom informs us in this little rhyme,
That little by little will work every time.

AWARD-WINNING
AUTHOR

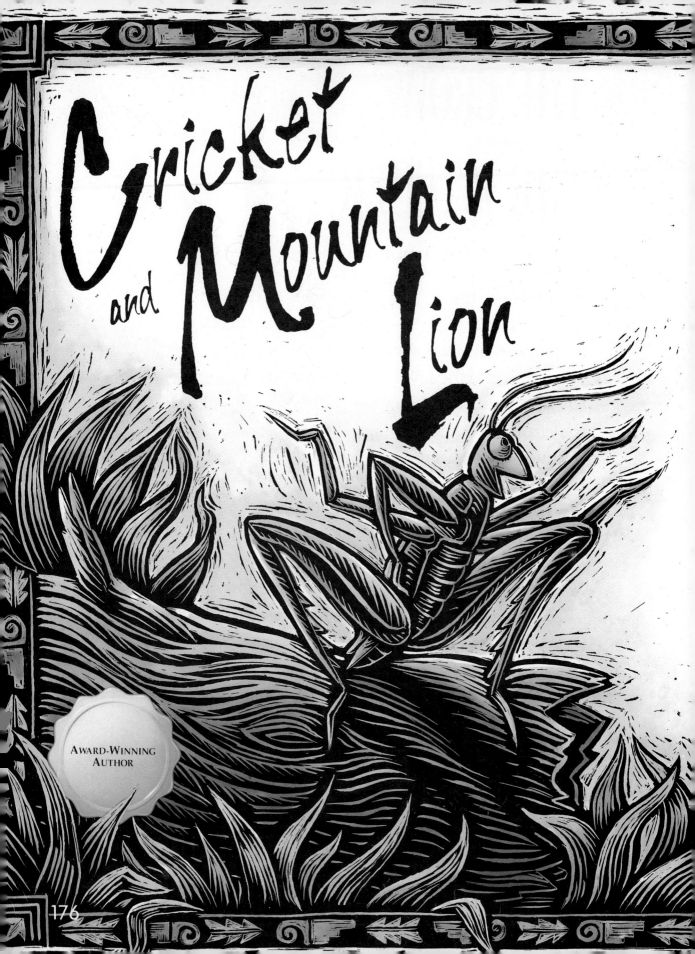

Cricket and Mountain Lion

AWARD-WINNING AUTHOR

Cricket was proud of his
house. It was small and round
and snug, and sat in a shady spot safely
away from the deer trail. Cricket had built
it himself of mud and dung and fine grass, then
rolled it into place beside a rotten log, and settled in.

One day Mountain Lion, out hunting, came
stepping softly down the deer trail. Not far from
Cricket's house his nose told him that a rabbit had crossed
the path a moment before, and so he turned aside. As he
padded past the rotten log, Mountain Lion heard a tiny shout.

"Hai, friend Lion! Stop where you are and step aside!
That is my house. One step more and your paw will crush it."

from *Back in the Beforetime: Tales of the California Indians*
retold by Jane Louise Curry ● illustrated by Jennifer Hewitson

Mountain Lion looked around to see who had spoken. When he spied little Cricket atop the log, he laughed. And then he roared until the leaves on the trees trembled.

"Miserable little creature!" he screamed. "Do *you* mean to tell *me* where I may walk? I am Mountain Lion. Not even Eagle can command me. Because I am strong and smart and swift, the forest is mine. And yet you dare to tell me where to step!"

"You may rule the forest, Big Paws," piped Cricket, "but I am Chief in my house and ruler of the land it sits on. So step aside. I do not care to have my house flattened."

Mountain Lion was amazed at Cricket's daring. "Indeed!" roared he. "I will flatten it and you too, if I wish. If I wish, little squeaker, I can crush you and all your folk under my paw."

Cricket gave an angry hop. "Hai, you think so? Take care. I may be small but I have a cousin not half so big as I am who is a great fighter. He can master a Grizzly Bear. So take care!"

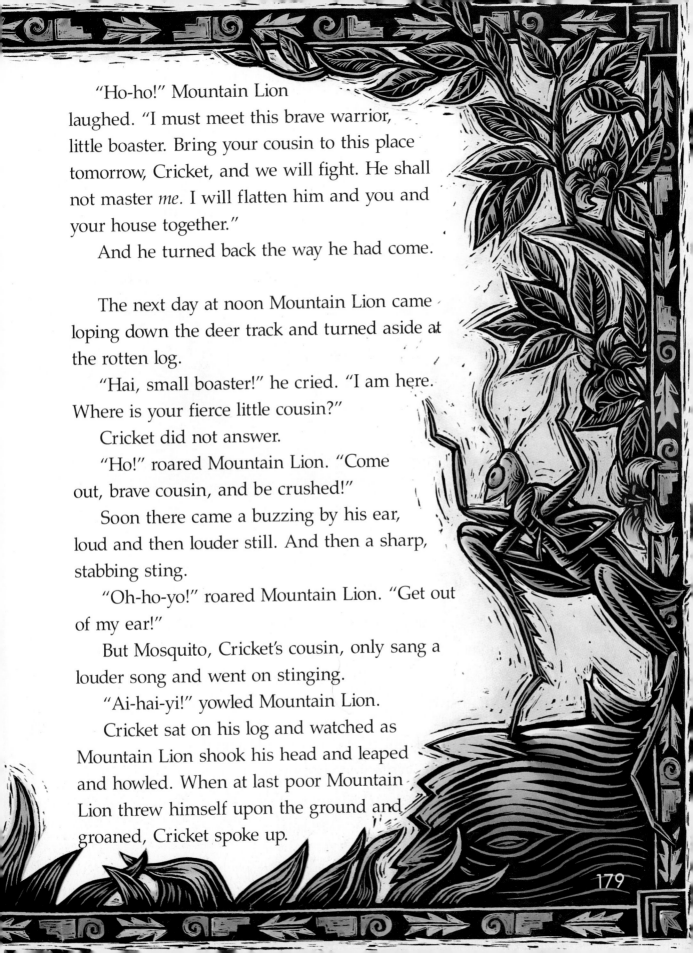

"Ho-ho!" Mountain Lion laughed. "I must meet this brave warrior, little boaster. Bring your cousin to this place tomorrow, Cricket, and we will fight. He shall not master *me*. I will flatten him and you and your house together."

And he turned back the way he had come.

The next day at noon Mountain Lion came loping down the deer track and turned aside at the rotten log.

"Hai, small boaster!" he cried. "I am here. Where is your fierce little cousin?"

Cricket did not answer.

"Ho!" roared Mountain Lion. "Come out, brave cousin, and be crushed!"

Soon there came a buzzing by his ear, loud and then louder still. And then a sharp, stabbing sting.

"Oh-ho-yo!" roared Mountain Lion. "Get out of my ear!"

But Mosquito, Cricket's cousin, only sang a louder song and went on stinging.

"Ai-hai-yi!" yowled Mountain Lion.

Cricket sat on his log and watched as Mountain Lion shook his head and leaped and howled. When at last poor Mountain Lion threw himself upon the ground and groaned, Cricket spoke up.

"Tell me, friend Lion. Do you mean to leave me and my house alone?"

"I will, I will, dear Cricket," moaned Mountain Lion. "Only call your cousin out of my ear."

So Cricket called Mosquito, and they sat together on the log and laughed to see Mountain Lion run away as fast as he could go.

He never ever came back.

If you were Mountain Lion, would you come back? Tell why or why not.

At the beginning of the story, Mountain Lion laughs at tiny Cricket. Do you think Cricket and Mosquito have "the last laugh"? Explain your answer.

WRITE Think about the moral or lesson this tale teaches. Write it in your own words.

Being Clever

Think about a clever character from one of your favorite stories or movies. How is the character like the characters in the stories you have just read?

WRITER'S WORKSHOP

Write your own story about a clever person or animal. Make sure that your story has a beginning, a middle, and an ending.

Writer's Choice: You have read about being clever. You might want to write about a person or an animal that is special in some other way. You might want to write about something else. Plan what you will write and how you will share it.

THEME

Using Your Wits

How do you solve problems or puzzles? Some solutions are easy to find. For others, you have to try and try again. See whether you can figure out the solutions as you read the mysterious stories that follow.

CONTENTS

THE PIZZA

AWARD-WINNING
AUTHORS

MONSTER

by Marjorie and Mitchell Sharmat

Who should you call when you're in trouble?

Olivia Sharp. That's me.

My friends call me Olivia.

My enemies call me Liver.

I have a best friend, Taffy Plimpton. But she moved away to Carmel. The next day I went out and got an owl named Hoot. She promised me she wouldn't move away.

Hoot and I live in a penthouse at the top of Pacific Heights with my chauffeur, Willie, my housekeeper, Mrs. Fridgeflake, and my folks.

But my folks aren't home much. This month they're in Paris.

Mrs. Fridgeflake is home all the time. But as far as I'm concerned, she might as well be in Paris. She's always busy flicking specks from glasses, fluffing pillows, and waxing plants.

Our penthouse has twelve bedrooms. I use two of them. One to be myself in and one to be a special agent in.

I have three telephones, one of them red.

I wasn't always a special agent. After Taffy moved away, I used to sit around a lot in my furry white chair and look out my huge living room window at the boats going back and forth on San Francisco Bay.

Fantastic view.

But even when I looked at it with Hoot on my shoulder, I still felt lonely.

I'd never tell anybody that!

It was my secret.

My problem.

One night I said to Hoot, "I bet there must be a trillion secret problems out there. Waiting to be solved."

I'm good at solving problems, except for my own.

I'm good at keeping secrets, too.

I kept talking to Hoot. "If you're good at something, you shouldn't waste it, right?"

Hoot looked at me, silent but wise.

I could tell her answer was a definite YES.

And that's when I, Olivia Sharp, got into the agent business.

The next day I had Willie drive me to a print shop.

I had some ads printed up.

They all said:

DO YOU HAVE A
SECRET PROBLEM?

ARE YOU IN TROUBLE?

DO YOU NEED HELP?

YOU NEED ME.

CALL OLIVIA SHARP
Agent for Secrets
555–4848

Willie and I put up the ads around the city.

On telephone poles.

On street signs.

In store windows.

At the post office.

On school bulletin boards.

Everywhere!

Then I hooked up my special red telephone and I was ready for business.

I was setting up my files when I got my first call.

I answered immediately.

"Olivia Sharp, Agent for Secrets, here," I said.

I heard a sigh.

Then a voice said, "The world is coming to an end."

It was Duncan. I knew him from school.

"The world is coming to an end," he said again.

"That's what you always say." I strung three paper clips together. Why was he bothering me!

"I saw your ad at the pizza store," he said. "Can you help me?"

"I can't stop the world from coming to an end," I told him. "I'm good, but not that good."

"You don't understand," Duncan said. "I lost my best friend. Don't tell anybody."

"I'm good at keeping secrets," I said. "Stay put. I'll be right over."

I slammed down the receiver and rang for Willie to bring the limo around.

Then I went to the closet and got my boa.

When I hit the street, Willie was waiting with the limo. "Where to, Miss Olivia?" he asked.

"To Duncan's, and hurry. It's an emergency."

"You've got it, Boss," said Willie as we rolled out of the courtyard and through the big iron gates leading onto Steiner Street.

While we rode up and down the hills to Duncan's flat, I remembered something. Duncan didn't *have* any friends. So how could he lose his best one? Duncan is *so* depressing. He's always saying that the world is coming to an end. And nobody likes to hear that. I know I don't, but a client is a client.

When we got to Duncan's, I told Willie to wait. I should have told him to give me a piggyback ride. Duncan lives in a flat on the fourth floor of a walk-up.

I was out of breath when I knocked on Duncan's door.

He answered it.

Duncan's hair was hanging over his eyes as if half his face was hiding from the world. His socks drooped over his sneakers, and his baggy blue jeans were slipping over his hips.

All of Duncan seemed to be on the way down. This guy was a real downer all right!

"Where did you lose this best friend of yours, and who is he?" I asked Duncan.

"It's Desiree, and I lost her inside Angelo's Pizza Parlor," he said.

"That's only around the corner," I said. "How could you lose her there?"

"We went into Angelo's to get pizza. I ordered a slice for her and a slice for me. When the slices came, I handed Desiree one of them. And that's when I lost her."

"You gave Desiree a slice of pizza and she disappeared? Did she go in a puff of garlic or something?"

I laughed and fluffed my boa.

Duncan never laughs. What with the world coming to an end and all that rot.

He said, "Desiree didn't even eat her slice. She got mad and left the pizza parlor. That's how I lost my best friend."

Duncan pulled something out of his pocket.

"I saved her slice. Want it?"

Duncan dangled a limp little piece of cold pizza right under my nose.

I stepped backward.

Then I looked down at the pizza.

"This slice is very small," I said. "Was the one you kept for yourself bigger?"

Duncan shrugged. "I didn't measure them. I ate mine up and then I went home and called Desiree. But she hung up on me."

"Maybe you can get another friend. On second thought, that's not likely. I've got it. Get another pizza—a whole one—and give it to Desiree."

Duncan's face dropped. It was always doing that. "I'm out of money. I spent my last cent at Angelo's."

"Never fear, Olivia's here." I opened my purse and peeled off a ten-dollar bill. "This should cover it. Go back to Angelo's immediately and order a pizza to go. A large pizza with everything on it. Tie a huge red ribbon around the box. Take it to Desiree's house and give it to her. I'm glad I could help."

I went back downstairs to Willie and the limo. It was a lot easier walking down than climbing up.

I always feel I deserve a small reward when I've helped someone. I had Willie take us to the Bon Ton Chocolate Shop for two of their superdooper ice-cream sodas.

When I got home, my red phone was ringing.

It was Duncan.

"How did it go?" I asked.

"Disasterville," he said. "Desiree said the ribbon was pretty. While she was untying it, I told her what was inside the box. Then suddenly she gave me a weird look and shoved the box back at me."

I had had the ice-cream soda too soon.

Duncan was still talking. "The box split open. The pizza slid out. Now I still have no best friend and I'm smeared from head to toe with tomato sauce, cheese, mushrooms, and anchovies. I look like a gooey pizza monster!"

I could almost see Duncan dripping pizza stuff. When I started in this agent business, I never expected to have a

pizza monster for my first client. But I stayed cool. "I'll think of something else," I said. "You can depend upon Olivia Sharp."

"Hurry! The world is coming to an end," Duncan said, and he hung up.

I went to the window and looked out at the bay. A garbage barge was going by.

I knew what had gone wrong. How could I expect just one pizza, even with everything on it, to solve Duncan's problem?

I looked up Desiree's address.

I rang for Willie.

"Willie," I said, "find the name of a pizza bakery, and order fifty different kinds of pizzas to be sent to Desiree. Enclose a card saying *I hope you like one of these. From your best friend, Duncan.*"

"You've got it, Boss," Willie said.

That should take care of that, I thought. It's nice to be really, really rich and able to help others.

I stuck my feet up in the air.

I painted my toenails and wiggled them dry.

I fed Hoot.

Sometimes she hoots.

Sometimes she doesn't.

Sometimes I'm as wise as she is.

Sometimes I'm not.

I was in the bathtub when the red telephone rang.

I grabbed my robe, rushed to my office, answered my phone, and heard, "The world has now come to an end."

It was Duncan, of course.

"Tell me about it," I said.

"Desiree just called me. She's madder than ever. She said she doesn't want fifty pizzas. What does she mean?"

"No problem," I said to him. "I'll look into it."

I hung up.

I had a real problem, but I never admit that to a client. Desiree had turned down a slice of pizza, a whole pizza, and now fifty pizzas. And she was very mad. There had to be more to this than a too-small slice of pizza!

I got dressed and rang for Willie to bring the limo around.

"To Desiree's place," I said.

When we got to Desiree's apartment house, we couldn't find a place to park, so I told Willie to circle the block.

Five circles later, I was out of the car and heading toward Desiree's front door. She lives on the ground floor.

The fifty pizzas were blocking the way.

I picked my way through them.

I pounded on Desiree's door.

She opened it.

Desiree turned out to be one of those perfect scrub-a-dub-dub blondes who ties her hair back in a ponytail with a rainbow-colored ribbon. Without looking down I knew she'd be wearing shiny patent-leather, pointy-toed shoes that she could tippy-tap across the room in. I could see why Duncan liked her. Myself, I can't stand the type.

"I'm here about Duncan," I said, handing her my card.

Olivia Sharp
AGENT FOR SECRETS
I CAN FIX ANYTHING.
555-4848

I stuck my foot inside her door while I spoke. I wasn't
going to take any chance she'd slam the door in my face
when she heard why I was there. That's a trick we agents
have.

"Come in," Desiree said without noticing that I was
already partway in.

I flung my boa on the sofa in her living room.

I said, "Duncan hired me to find his lost best friend.
You. Don't you know it's wrong to get angry about a slice
of pizza?"

I knew that wasn't why Desiree was mad at Duncan. I
was fishing. Secret agents have to do that.

"The pizza was just an excuse," Desiree said. "I don't
want to be Duncan's friend. He's so . . . so . . ."

"Depressing?" I offered. "Totally, totally depressing?"

"Right," Desiree said. "He's no fun at all."

"So why did you go into Angelo's Pizza Parlor with him?"

"He came along just as I was going inside. He said, 'Getting a piece of pizza? Me too.' So we went in together. When our slices came, he handed me one."

"And?"

"He said, 'Have a piece of this gucky, yucky, slimy pizza, which has dead cheese and dying mushrooms on it.' That's why I left. Do you blame me?"

Desiree didn't expect an answer. She folded my boa neatly and went on talking.

"Later on, Duncan brought a whole pizza to my house in a box tied with a pretty red ribbon. While I was untying the ribbon he said, 'Here's the slimiest pizza with all the guckiest, yuckiest things in the world on it. It probably died on the way over.'"

"That sounds like Duncan," I said.

"Yes," Desiree said. "He can even make Angelo's pizza look disgusting. Who needs a friend like that?"

Nobody, I thought. That was the whole trouble. Nobody.

I took a hard look at Desiree. She was tugging at her ribbon. Her rainbow was unraveling. Duncan can do that to you. Unravel rainbows and all of that.

But he was my client.

I knew what I had to do.

I grabbed my boa. "I must dash off," I said.

I left.

At the front door, the neighborhood dogs and cats were gathering around the pizzas.

"Feast!" I called as I got into my limo.

"To the main library," I said to Willie.

The library has absolutely tons and tons of books. Willie whisked me there.

I checked out ten jokebooks.

"To Duncan's," I said to Willie.

When we got to Duncan's building, Willie helped me carry the ten books up to the fourth floor.

Duncan opened the door on the first knock.

We handed him the books.

"Here. Read these!" I gasped while I tried to catch my breath.

Then Willie and I took off.

When I got home, my red telephone was ringing.

I rushed to answer it.

But I was too late. No one was there.

I flung myself on the couch in my office. This was an exhausting case.

The red telephone rang again.

Duncan was on the line.

"Where have you been?" he asked. "I've been calling and calling. Why did you bring me these dopey jokebooks?"

"To put a smile on your face."

"A smile?" he asked.

"Yes, a smile. That nice curvy thing under the nose that most kids have when they think cheery thoughts. Which, by the way, you never do."

"But you're supposed to help me with Desiree."

"Duncan, darling, Desiree's mad at you because you said awful things about the pizza. You say awful things all the time about *everything*. That's why Desiree doesn't want to be your friend."

"Are you sure?"

"Positive. Listen to me, Duncan. You just said the books I gave you are dopey. Have you even *read* them?"

"No."

"See what I mean? Now I've got something important for you to do, Duncan. Go to your window, look out, and tell me if you can see the world coming to an end."

"Hold on," Duncan said.

He put the receiver down.

I waited.

I tapped my fingers on my desk.

It was taking Duncan forever.

How big a job could it be?

At last he came back to the phone.

"I looked north and I looked south," he said, "but I didn't actually *see* the world coming to an end. I couldn't see east or west because there are buildings in the way."

"Believe me," I said, "east and west are in good shape. I checked on them. Okay?"

"Okay," Duncan said. "So the world isn't coming to an end. But what do I do about Desiree?"

"Think happy. Read the jokebooks I gave you. Find a joke you really, really adore. Then call up Desiree and tell it to her fast before she can hang up on you. Then call me back."

I slammed down the receiver.

I waited for Duncan to call back.

I read my horoscope.

I arranged my credit cards in alphabetical order.

I smoothed Hoot's feathers.

The red telephone rang.

Duncan was on the line, laughing.

Laughing!

"I found five great jokes," he said. "Desiree listened to all of them, and she laughed."

"Super," I said.

"She says she's thinking about being my friend."

"Now you're getting somewhere," I said. "All you have to do is keep it up. You don't need me anymore."

"You know Desiree was never my best friend," Duncan said.

"I know it."

"*You* are!" he said.

"Not yet," I said.

I put down the receiver.

I made some notes for my files.

I closed my files and turned out the light in my office.

I went into my other bedroom to be myself.

Tomorrow I'm going to school. Sometimes I'm a regular kid. Sometimes I'm not.

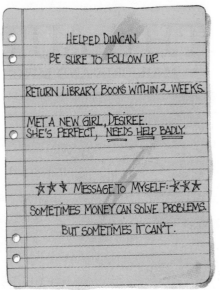

HELPED DUNCAN.

BE SURE TO FOLLOW UP.

RETURN LIBRARY BOOKS WITHIN 2 WEEKS.

MET A NEW GIRL, DESIREE. SHE'S PERFECT, NEEDS HELP BADLY.

★★★ MESSAGE TO MYSELF: ★★★ SOMETIMES MONEY CAN SOLVE PROBLEMS. BUT SOMETIMES IT CAN'T.

Would you hire Olivia to solve a problem? Why or why not?

Olivia writes in her notes, "Sometimes money can solve problems. But sometimes it can't." How does the case teach her this?

What traits make Olivia a good secret agent? Explain your answer.

WRITE   Imagine you are looking for a secret agent. Make a list of the things you will look for in a person before you hire him or her.

THE AUTHORS:

MARJORIE AND MITCHELL SHARMAT

Have you ever wondered what your family tree looks like? I mean, the real lowdown on your parents? What your great-grandparents were like? That kind of thing. Well, I did, and since I'm sort of a detective, I decided to do a deep background check on where I came from.

It didn't take me long. I went to the library and looked up my name. There I was in big letters: OLIVIA SHARP.

I was born in 1987 in Tucson, Arizona. The brain-child of Mitchell and Marjorie Sharmat. They have many other children. Two of them are real, and hundreds of them are fictional, just like me. Maybe you know Mitchell's Gregory, the Terrible Eater, or Marjorie's Nate the Great?

The Sharmats tried hard to pick the right name for me. First, Mitchell thought of Gertrude Gumshoe (awful, huh?). Then there were Jennifer, Danielle, Tiffany, Nicole, Stephanie, and plenty of others, including Bianca Bunko (*really* awful!). Finally . . . Olivia Sharp, and they knew it was the real me.

The Sharmats decided that I should live in San Francisco, in a penthouse, and that I should travel around in a limo. The Sharmats went to San Francisco, hired a limo, scouted the neighborhood where they thought I should live and go to school. They even found a pizza parlor for *The Pizza Monster.*

AWARD-WINNING
AUTHORS

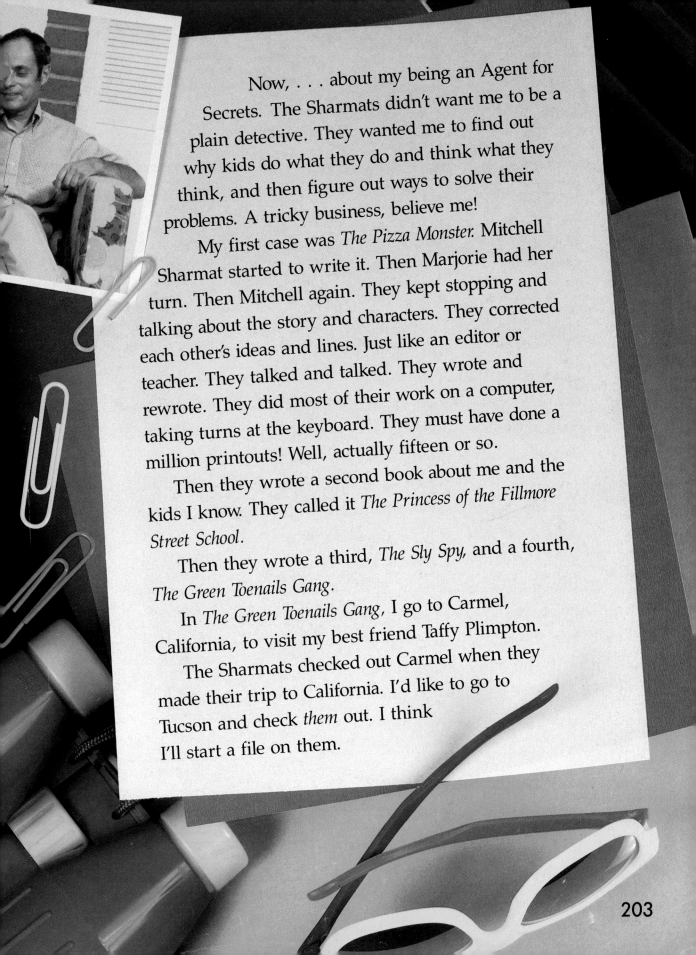

Now, . . . about my being an Agent for Secrets. The Sharmats didn't want me to be a plain detective. They wanted me to find out why kids do what they do and think what they think, and then figure out ways to solve their problems. A tricky business, believe me!

My first case was *The Pizza Monster.* Mitchell Sharmat started to write it. Then Marjorie had her turn. Then Mitchell again. They kept stopping and talking about the story and characters. They corrected each other's ideas and lines. Just like an editor or teacher. They talked and talked. They wrote and rewrote. They did most of their work on a computer, taking turns at the keyboard. They must have done a million printouts! Well, actually fifteen or so.

Then they wrote a second book about me and the kids I know. They called it *The Princess of the Fillmore Street School.*

Then they wrote a third, *The Sly Spy,* and a fourth, *The Green Toenails Gang.*

In *The Green Toenails Gang,* I go to Carmel, California, to visit my best friend Taffy Plimpton.

The Sharmats checked out Carmel when they made their trip to California. I'd like to go to Tucson and check *them* out. I think I'll start a file on them.

CHOCOLATE CHIP COOKIE Caper

by Susannah Brin and Nancy Sundquist

One summer day, Grandma Jane decided to wash her kitchen floor. The floor had gotten dirty earlier when she had made chocolate chip cookies. "Oh well, the cookie jar is full now and I have a few left over for my neighbor," said Grandma Jane to herself. After washing the floor, Grandma Jane decided to take her neighbor the plate of extra cookies while the floor dried. She closed the kitchen window and locked the back door. On the way to the neighbor's, she passed Tony the gardener. Tony was planting seeds in the flower bed. Then she passed three-year-old Buddy Sullivan playing in his plastic swimming pool. Grandma Jane gave both Tony and Buddy a chocolate chip cookie.

Later when Grandma Jane returned home, she found that someone had been in her kitchen. Look at the picture below of Grandma Jane's kitchen. The clues in the story and the clues in the picture will help you solve the mystery. Answer the following questions:

❶ How did the thief enter the kitchen?

❷ What did the thief steal?

❸ Who was the thief?

❹ How do you know who the thief was?

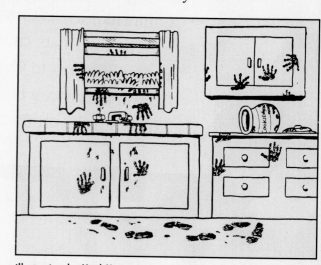

illustration by Neal Yamamoto

Using Your Wits

Think about the mysterious events in "The Pizza Monster" and "Chocolate Chip Cookie Caper." What clues did the authors give to help you solve the mysteries? Which mystery was easier to solve? Why?

WRITER'S WORKSHOP

Choose an animal or a thing that you can watch closely. Write a descriptive paragraph about what you see and notice. Use words to paint a colorful picture in your reader's mind.

Writer's Choice:
You have read about people who use their wits to solve mysteries. You might want to write about a person who uses his or her wits to do something else. Choose a way to share your writing.

CONNECTIONS

Multicultural Connection

Mayan Mystery

What caused the disappearance of people from the Mayan cities? This is one of the great puzzles of all time. More than a thousand years ago, the Maya built large stone cities in Mexico and Central America. They also developed writing and math skills. Then, several hundred years later, they suddenly left their cities.

What happened? Experts once believed that wars or natural disasters caused the people to leave. Now, many people think there may have been food shortages and revolts by the people against their rulers. Still, we may never know the whole truth.

In a small group, prepare a report on an ancient Mayan city. Present your report to your classmates, using pictures or models if possible.

Chichén Itzá, Mexico

Mayan Ruins

Tikal Calendar

Science/Math Connection

Calendar Symbols

The Maya developed a calendar. They used eighteen months of twenty days each, plus an extra five days at the end of the year. Create your own calendar, showing twelve months. Use a different drawing or design for each month. Share your calendar with your classmates.

Palenque, Mexico

Social Studies Connection

Lost Cities

With a partner or small group, find out about another culture's "lost" city, such as Machu Picchu in Peru or Pueblo Bonito in New Mexico. List the interesting facts you find, and give a short report to your classmates.

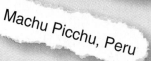
Machu Picchu, Peru

UNIT THREE 3

Memories

*A hundred thousand years have passed
Yet, I hear the distant beat of my
  father's drums.*

Shirley Daniels

Did you know that Matthew A.
Henson was an explorer or that Ida
B. Wells was a newspaper writer?
These are two people who helped
build America. The people who
have been important to our
country's growth are not always
remembered by name. But the
traditions they brought to America
will never be forgotten. As you read
this unit, think about the values that
helped shape this country.

BOOKSHELF

THE NEWS ABOUT DINOSAURS

by Patricia Lauber

This book presents new discoveries and ideas about dinosaurs. Were they quick and agile, or slow and clumsy? Did some have feathers? Find out the latest answers.

SLJ Best Books of the Year, Outstanding Science Trade Book

Harcourt Brace Library Book

THE KEEPING QUILT

by Patricia Polacco

A quilt becomes a "keeping quilt" when it is passed from mother to daughter for almost one hundred years. The quilt is used as a Sabbath tablecloth, a wedding canopy, and a baby blanket.

Teachers' Choice

Harcourt Brace Library Book

IN COAL COUNTRY

written by Judith Hendershot
illustrated by Thomas B. Allen

This beautifully illustrated book tells about the
excitement and hard work that go along with
growing up in a coal-mining community.
ALA Notable Book, Boston Globe–Horn Book
Honor, New York Times Best Illustrated
Books of the Year

MANDY

written by Barbara D. Booth

Mandy has a special relationship with her
grandmother. They make cookies, walk in the woods,
and dance together. Then something happens that
forces Mandy outside on a dark, stormy night.
Teachers' Choice

ROXABOXEN

written by Alice McLerran
illustrated by Barbara Cooney

Welcome to Roxaboxen. It's a town made of rocks,
pebbles, and old wooden boxes. It has dishes made
from pieces of pottery and horses made from sticks.
It's a special place!
Award-Winning Illustrator

THEME

Remembering

Some families pass along objects and customs to other family members. Passing along things and ideas is a way of keeping memories alive. The following stories and poems show how the past can be remembered.

CONTENTS

213

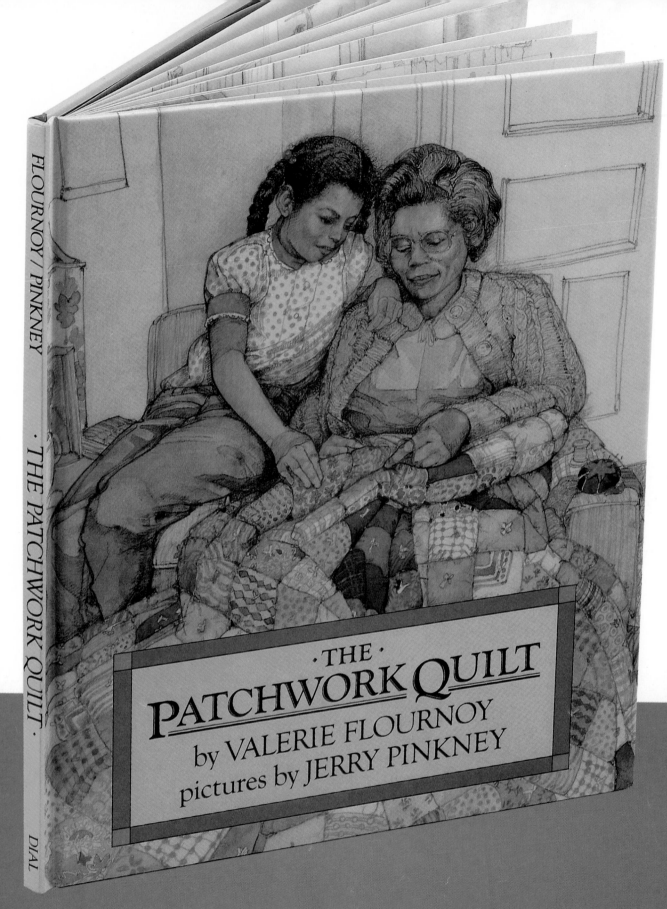

THE · PATCHWORK QUILT

by VALERIE FLOURNOY
pictures by JERRY PINKNEY

Tanya sat restlessly on her chair by the kitchen window. For several days she had had to stay in bed with a cold. But now Tanya's cold was almost gone. She was anxious to go outside and enjoy the fresh air and the arrival of spring.

"Mama, when can I go outside?" asked Tanya. Mama pulled the tray of biscuits from the oven and placed it on the counter.

"In time," she murmured. "All in good time."

Tanya gazed through the window and saw her two brothers, Ted and Jim, and Papa building the new backyard fence.

"I'm gonna talk to Grandma," she said.

ALA NOTABLE BOOK

CHILDREN'S CHOICE

CORETTA SCOTT KING AWARD

Grandma was sitting in her favorite spot—the big soft chair in front of the picture window. In her lap were scraps of materials of all textures and colors. Tanya recognized some of them. The plaid was from Papa's old work shirt, and the red scraps were from the shirt Ted had torn that winter.

"Whatcha gonna do with all that stuff?" Tanya asked.

"Stuff? These ain't stuff. These little pieces gonna make me a quilt, a patchwork quilt."

Tanya tilted her head. "I know what a quilt is, Grandma. There's one on your bed, but it's old and dirty and Mama can never get it clean."

Grandma sighed. "It ain't dirty, honey. It's worn, the way it's supposed to be."

Grandma flexed her fingers to keep them from stiffening. She sucked in some air and said, "My mother made me a quilt when I wasn't any older than you. But sometimes the old ways are forgotten."

Tanya leaned against the chair and rested her head on her grandmother's shoulder.

Just then Mama walked in with two glasses of milk and some biscuits. Mama looked at the scraps of material that were scattered all over. "Grandma," she said, "I just cleaned this room, and now it's a mess."

"It's not a mess, Mama," Tanya said through a mouthful of biscuit. "It's a quilt."

"A quilt! You don't need these scraps. I can get you a quilt," Mama said.

Grandma looked at her daughter and then turned to her grandchild. "Yes, your mama can get you a quilt from any department store. But it won't be like my patchwork quilt, and it won't last as long either."

Mama looked at Grandma, then picked up Tanya's empty glass and went to make lunch.

Grandma's eyes grew dark and distant. She turned away from Tanya and gazed out the window, absentmindedly rubbing the pieces of material through her fingers.

"Grandma, I'll help you make your quilt," Tanya said.

"Thank you, honey."

"Let's start right now. We'll be finished in no time."

Grandma held Tanya close and patted her head. "It's gonna take quite a while to make this quilt, not a couple of days or a week—not even a month. A good quilt, a masterpiece . . ." Grandma's eyes shone at the thought. "Why I need more material. More gold and blue, some red and green. And I'll need the time to do it right. It'll take me a year at least."

"A year," shouted Tanya. "That's too long. I can't wait that long, Grandma."

Grandma laughed. "A year ain't that long, honey. Makin' this quilt gonna be a joy. Now run along and let Grandma rest." Grandma turned her head toward the sunlight and closed her eyes.

"I'm gonna make a masterpiece," she murmured, clutching a scrap of cloth in her hand, just before she fell asleep.

"We'll have to get you a new pair and use these old ones for rags," Mama said as she hung the last piece of wash on the clothesline one August afternoon.

Jim was miserable. His favorite blue corduroy pants had been held together with patches; now they were beyond repair.

"Bring them here," Grandma said.

Grandma took part of the pant leg and cut a few blue squares. Jim gave her a hug and watched her add his patches to the others.

"A quilt won't forget. It can tell your life story," she said.

The arrival of autumn meant school and
Halloween. This year Tanya would be an African
princess. She danced around in the long, flowing
robes Mama had made from several yards of colorful
material. The old bracelets and earrings Tanya had
found in a trunk in the attic jingled noisily as she
moved. Grandma cut some squares out of the
leftover scraps and added Tanya to the quilt too!

The days grew colder but Tanya and her brothers didn't mind. They knew snow wasn't far away. Mama dreaded winter's coming. Every year she would plead with Grandma to move away from the drafty window, but Grandma wouldn't budge.

"Grandma, please," Mama scolded. "You can sit here by the heater."

"I'm not your grandmother, I'm your mother," Grandma said. "And I'm gonna sit here in the Lord's light and make my masterpiece."

It was the end of November when Ted, Jim, and Tanya got their wish. They awoke one morning to find everything in sight covered with snow. Tanya got dressed and flew down the stairs. Ted and Jim, and even Mama and Papa, were already outside.

"I don't like leaving Grandma in that house by herself," Mama said. "I know she's lonely."

Tanya pulled herself out of the snow being careful not to ruin her angel. "Grandma isn't lonely," Tanya said happily. "She and the quilt are telling each other stories."

Mama glanced questioningly at Tanya, "Telling each other stories?"

"Yes, Grandma says a quilt never forgets!"

The family spent the morning and most of the afternoon sledding down the hill. Finally, when they were all numb from the cold, they went inside for hot chocolate and sandwiches.

"I think I'll go sit and talk to Grandma," Mama said.

"Then she can explain to you about our quilt—our very own family quilt," Tanya said.

Mama saw the mischievous glint in her youngest child's eyes.

"Why, I may just have her do that, young lady," Mama said as she walked out of the kitchen.

Tanya leaned over the table to see into the living room. Grandma was hunched over, her eyes close to the fabric as she made tiny stitches. Mama sat at the old woman's feet. Tanya couldn't hear what was said but she knew Grandma was telling Mama all about quilts and how *this* quilt would be very special. Tanya sipped her chocolate slowly, then she saw Mama pick up a piece of fabric, rub it with her fingers, and smile.

From that moment on both women spent their winter evenings working on the quilt. Mama did the sewing while Grandma cut the fabrics and placed the scraps in a pattern of colors. Even while they were cooking and baking all their Christmas specialties during the day, at night they still worked on the quilt. Only once did Mama put it aside. She wanted to wear something special Christmas night, so she bought some gold material and made a beautiful dress. Tanya knew without asking that the gold scraps would be in the quilt too.

There was much singing and laughing that Christmas. All Grandma's sons and daughters and nieces and nephews came to pay their respects. The Christmas tree lights shone brightly, filling the room with sparkling colors. Later, when everyone had gone home, Papa said he had never felt so much happiness in the house. And Mama agreed.

When Tanya got downstairs the next morning, she found Papa fixing pancakes.

"Is today a special day too?" asked Jim.

"Where's Mama?" asked Tanya.

"Grandma doesn't feel well this morning," Papa said. "Your mother is with her now till the doctor gets here."

"Will Grandma be all right?" Ted asked.

Papa rubbed his son's head and smiled. "There's nothing for you to worry about. We'll take care of Grandma."

Tanya looked into the living room. There on the back of the big chair rested the patchwork quilt. It was folded neatly, just as Grandma had left it.

"Mother didn't want us to know she wasn't feeling well. She thought it would spoil our Christmas," Mama told them later, her face drawn and tired, her eyes a puffy red. "Now it's up to all of us to be quiet and make her as comfortable as possible." Papa put an arm around Mama's shoulder.

"Can we see Grandma?" Tanya asked.

"No, not tonight," Papa said. "Grandma needs plenty of rest."

It was nearly a week, the day before New Year's, before the children were permitted to see their grandmother. She looked tired and spoke in whispers.

"We miss you, Grandma," Ted said.

"And your muffins and hot chocolate," added Jim. Grandma smiled.

"Your quilt misses you too, Grandma," Tanya said. Grandma's smile faded from her lips. Her eyes grew cloudy.

"My masterpiece," Grandma sighed. "It would have been beautiful. Almost half finished." The old woman closed her eyes and turned away from her grandchildren. Papa whispered it was time to leave. Ted, Jim, and Tanya crept from the room.

Tanya walked slowly to where the quilt lay. She had seen Grandma and Mama work on it. Tanya thought real hard. She knew how to cut the scraps, but she wasn't certain of the rest. Just then Tanya felt a hand resting on her shoulder. She looked up and saw Mama.

"Tomorrow," Mama said.

New Year's Day was the beginning. After the dishes were washed and put away, Tanya and Mama examined the quilt.

"You cut more squares, Tanya, while I stitch some patches together," Mama said.

Tanya snipped and trimmed the scraps of material till her hands hurt from the scissors. Mama watched her carefully, making sure the squares were all the same size. The next day was the same as the last. More snipping and cutting. But Mama couldn't always be around to watch Tanya work. Grandma had to be looked after. So Tanya worked by herself. Then one night, as Papa read them stories, Jim walked over and looked at the quilt. In it he saw patches of blue. His blue. Without saying a word Jim picked up the scissors and some scraps and started to make squares. Ted helped Jim put the squares in piles while Mama showed Tanya how to join them.

Every day, as soon as she got home from school,
Tanya worked on the quilt. Ted and Jim were too busy
with sports, and Mama was looking after Grandma, so
Tanya worked alone. But after a few weeks she
stopped. Something was wrong—something was
missing, Tanya thought. For days the quilt lay on the
back of the chair. No one knew why Tanya had stopped
working. Tanya would sit and look at the quilt. Finally
she knew. Some*thing* wasn't missing. Some*one* was
missing from the quilt.

That evening before she went to bed Tanya tiptoed
into Grandma's room, a pair of scissors in her hand.
She quietly lifted the end of Grandma's old quilt and
carefully removed a
few squares.

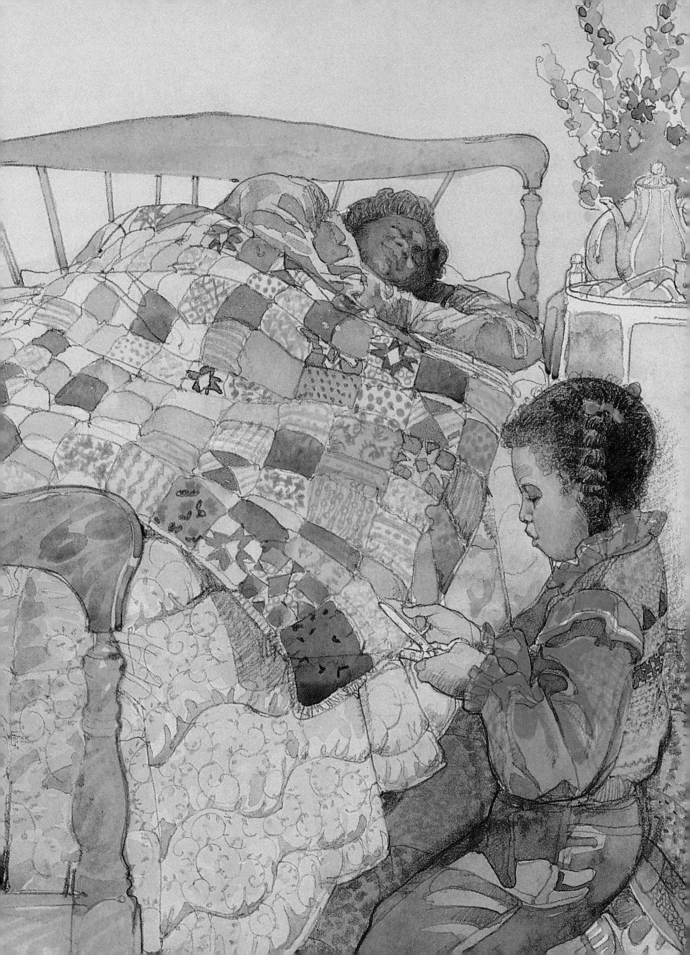

February and March came and went as Mama proudly watched her daughter work on the last few rows of patches. Tanya always found time for the quilt. Grandma had been watching too. The old woman had been getting stronger and stronger as the months passed. Once she was able, Papa would carry Grandma to her chair by the window. "I needs the Lord's light," Grandma said. Then she would sit and hum softly to herself and watch Tanya work.

"Yes, honey, this quilt is nothin' but a joy," Grandma said.

Summer vacation was almost here. One June day Tanya came home to find Grandma working on the quilt again! She had finished sewing the last few squares together; the stuffing was in place, and she was already pinning on the backing.

"Grandma!" Tanya shouted.

Grandma looked up. "Hush, child. It's almost time to do the quilting on these patches. But first I have some special finishing touches. . . ."

The next night Grandma cut the final thread with her teeth. "There. It's done," she said. Mama helped Grandma spread the quilt full length.

Nobody had realized how big it had gotten or how beautiful. Reds, greens, blues, and golds, light shades and dark, blended in and out throughout the quilt.

"It's beautiful," Papa said. He touched the gold patch, looked at Mama, and remembered. Jim remembered too. There was his blue and the red from Ted's shirt. There was Tanya's Halloween costume. And there was Grandma. Even though her patch was old, it fit right in.

241

They all remembered the past year. They especially remembered Tanya and all her work. So it had been decided. In the right hand corner of the last row of patches was delicately stitched, "For Tanya from your Mama and Grandma."

If you could, what would you like to help someone make? Give reasons for your answer.

The quilt took about one year to make. How did the author show you how much time had gone by?

WRITE Think of something you have made or would like to make. Write a letter to Tanya about it.

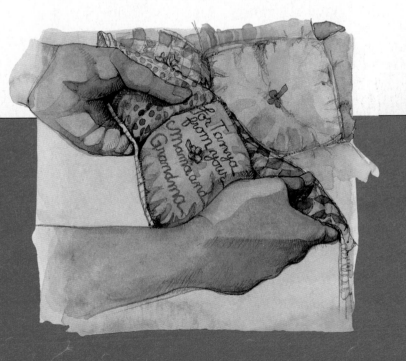

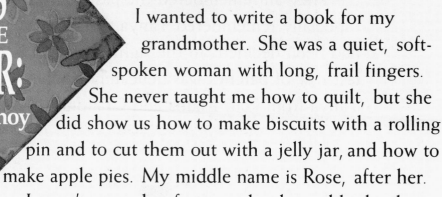

**AWARD-WINNING
AUTHOR**

I wrote *The Patchwork Quilt* because I wanted to write a book for my grandmother. She was a quiet, soft-spoken woman with long, frail fingers. She never taught me how to quilt, but she did show us how to make biscuits with a rolling pin and to cut them out with a jelly jar, and how to make apple pies. My middle name is Rose, after her.

I wasn't sure what form my book would take, but one day I was reading an article about quilting, and I decided that quilting would be a good way to talk about family history. Since I wrote this book, I've received lots of letters from kids and their parents who say the story reminds them of their family.

When I go to speak to people, they often bring in their old quilts. Sometimes the classes make their own quilts. They're made out of everything from tissue to felt. I don't quilt, but I've bought several books on quilting, and I'm going to take it up when I have a chance. Also, I've done some research on slavery, and I've learned that the slaves' quilts often contained messages with information about how to get away. That would make an interesting book.

People often think that authors and artists work together, but that's not always the case. The publisher of *The Patchwork Quilt* gave the manuscript to Jerry Pinkney, and I didn't see the pictures until the book was done. I thought they were wonderful! It was almost as if Jerry had been inside my mind and drew what I was able to see. Of all my books, *The Patchwork Quilt* is my favorite.

You have just read a story illustrated by Jerry Pinkney. Here's what Mr. Pinkney has to say about how he creates pictures for books.

AWARD-WINNING
ILLUSTRATOR

Question: Do you use models for the main characters in the books you illustrate?

Answer: Yes.

Question: Who were the models for the characters in *The Patchwork Quilt*?

Answer: I modeled the father in the story after myself. My wife, Gloria, was the model for Tanya's mother. The models for Tanya and her grandmother were two friends of mine, Shondell and Sophie.

Question: Did you have to do research to find out how Tanya's African princess costume should look?

Answer: Yes, I did research.

Question: Does an African princess really wear what Tanya wore?

Answer: The fabric for Tanya's costume is African.

Question: How did you decide on the illustration for the cover of the book?

Answer: I used the main characters in the story— Tanya and her grandmother—and the quilt, of course. I also tried to show the warmth and affection Tanya and her grandmother have for each other.

Question: What is the most enjoyable part of being a children's book illustrator?

Answer: For me it is when the art is finished and I receive the published book in the mail. It is very exciting to open a new book that I have illustrated.

245

THE PINE APPLE WOMEN
PAINT BY MR AMOS
FERGUSON 1986

THE PUMPKIN
MAN

THE CHICKEN
WOMEN

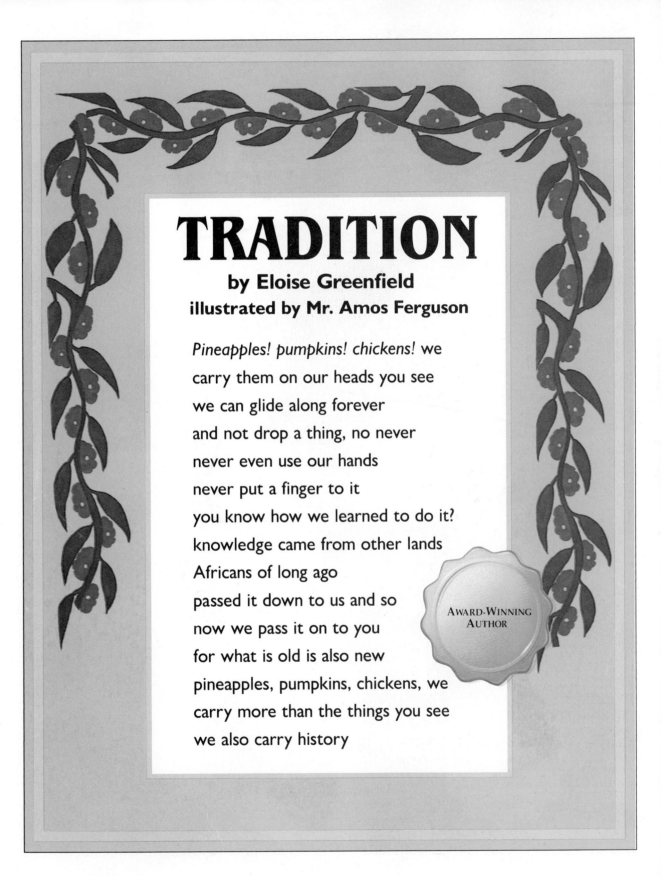

TRADITION

by Eloise Greenfield
illustrated by Mr. Amos Ferguson

Pineapples! pumpkins! chickens! we
carry them on our heads you see
we can glide along forever
and not drop a thing, no never
never even use our hands
never put a finger to it
you know how we learned to do it?
knowledge came from other lands
Africans of long ago
passed it down to us and so
now we pass it on to you
for what is old is also new
pineapples, pumpkins, chickens, we
carry more than the things you see
we also carry history

AWARD-WINNING
AUTHOR

SONG AND DANCE MAN

by
KAREN ACKERMAN

illustrated by
STEPHEN GAMMELL

Ackerman / Gammell

SONG AND DANCE MAN

CALDECOTT MEDAL
ALA NOTABLE
BOOK

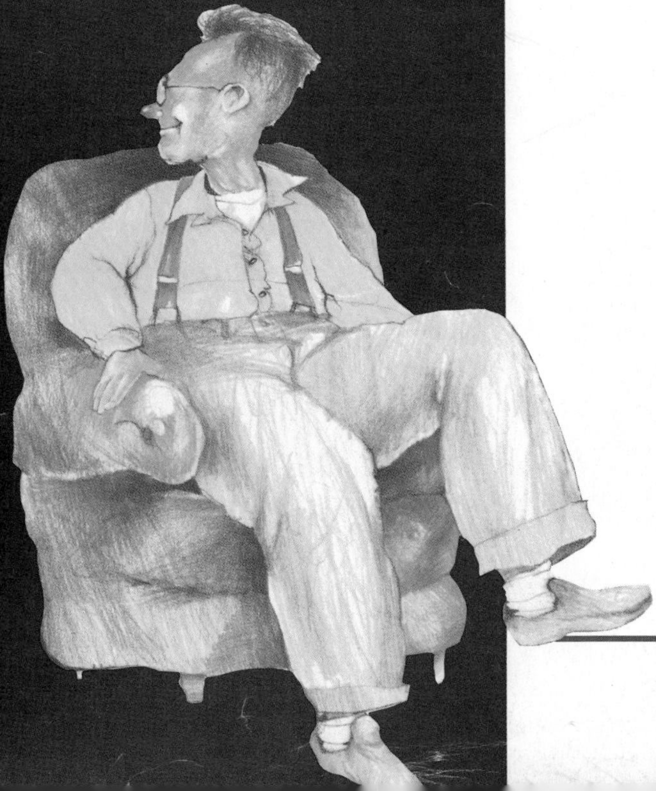

Grandpa was a song and dance man who once danced on the vaudeville stage.

When we visit, he tells us about a time before people watched TV, back in the good old days, the song and dance days.

"Supper in an hour!" Grandma calls from the kitchen.

"I wonder if my tap shoes still fit?" Grandpa says with a smile. Then he turns on the light to the attic, and we follow him up the steep, wooden steps.

Faded posters of Grandpa when he was young hang
on the walls. He moves some cardboard boxes and a rack
of Grandma's winter dresses out of the way, and we see a
dusty brown, leather-trimmed trunk in the corner.

As soon as Grandpa opens it, the smell of cedar chips
and old things saved fills the attic. Inside are his shoes
with the silver half-moon taps on the toes and heels,
bowler hats and top hats, and vests with stripes and
matching bow ties.

We try on the hats and pretend we're dancing on a vaudeville stage, where the bright lights twinkle and the piano player nods his head along with the music.

After wiping his shoes with a cloth he calls a shammy, Grandpa puts them on. He tucks small, white pads inside the shoes so his corns won't rub, and he turns on the lamps and aims each one down like a spotlight.

He sprinkles a little powder on the floor, and it's show time. We sit on one of Grandma's woolen blankets, clap our hands, and call out, "Yay, Grandpa!"

The song and dance man begins to dance the old soft shoe. His feet move slowly at first, while his tap shoes make soft, slippery sounds like rain on a tin roof.

We forget that it's Grandpa dancing, and all we can hear is the silvery tap of two feet, and all we can see is a song and dance man gliding across a vaudeville stage.

He says, "Watch this!" and does a new step that sounds like a woodpecker tapping on a tree. Suddenly, his shoes move faster, and he begins to sing. His voice is as round and strong as a canyon echo, and his cheeks get rosy as he sings "Yankee Doodle Boy," a song he knows from the good old days.

There are too many dance steps and too many words in the song for us to remember, but the show is better than any show on TV.

The song and dance man stops and leans forward with a wink.

"What's that in your ear?" he asks, and he pulls a silver dollar out of somebody's hair.

He rolls his bowler hat down his arm, catches it in his hand, and flips it back up onto his head.

"Know how to make an elephant float?" he asks. "One scoop of ice cream, two squirts of soda, and three scoops of elephant!"

We've heard that joke before, but the song and dance man slaps his knees and laughs until his eyes water.

He tries to wipe them with a red hanky from his vest pocket, but the hanky just gets longer and longer as he pulls it out. He looks so surprised that we start laughing too, and it feels like the whole attic is shaking.

Sometimes we laugh so hard, the hiccups start, and Grandpa stops to bring us a glass of water from the bathroom.

"Drink slow and hold your breath," he says, "or I'll have to scare you!"

Once our hiccups are gone, he gets a gold-tipped cane and a black silk top hat from the trunk. He lowers his eyes and tips the hat, and he's standing very still.

All the lights are turned low except one that shines on his polished tap shoes. It's the grand finale, so the song and dance man takes a deep breath. He lifts the cane and holds it in both hands.

Slowly, he starts to tap. His shoes move faster and faster, and the sounds coming from them are too many to make with only two feet.

He spins and jumps into the air. Touching the stage
again, he kneels with his arms spread out, and the silk
top hat and gold-tipped cane lie side by side at his feet.
His shoes are still, and the show is over.

We stand up together and clap our hands, shouting "Hurray!"
and "More!" but Grandpa only smiles and shakes his head,
all out of breath. He takes off his tap shoes, wraps them
gently in the shammy cloth, and puts them back in the leather-
trimmed trunk. He carefully folds his vest and lays the top hat
and cane on it, and we follow him to the stairway.

Grandpa holds on to the rail as we go down the steps.

At the bottom he hugs us, and we tell him we wish we
could have seen him dance in the good old days, the song and
dance days. He smiles, and whispers that he wouldn't trade a
million good old days for the days he spends with us.

But as he turns off the attic light, Grandpa glances back up
the stairs, and we wonder how much he really misses that time
on the vaudeville stage, when he was a song and dance man.

Do you think that a song and dance show could be better than any show on TV? Tell why or why not.

The children's grandpa has been in vaudeville. What have you learned about vaudeville from reading this story?

How do you know the children have seen Grandpa's act before?

WRITE Imagine that you are going to be in a song and dance show. Write a few sentences about your costume, the lighting, your songs and dances, and the audience.

DRUMS Of My FATHER

by Shirley Daniels △ illustrated by Robert Hunt

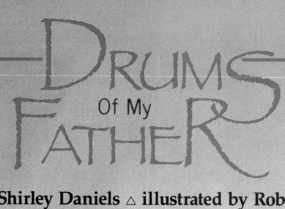

A hundred thousand years have passed
Yet, I hear the distant beat of my father's drums.
I hear his drums throughout the land,
His beat I feel within my heart.

The drums shall beat, so my heart shall beat,
And I shall live a hundred thousand years.

Remembering

In the stories and the poems you have just read, special memories are saved. Do you think it's important to remember the past? Why or why not?

WRITER'S WORKSHOP

Childhood toys and games often trigger happy memories. Write a thank-you note to a real or a make-believe friend, thanking him or her for a favorite gift or a special time.

Writer's Choice:
You might want to write something else about memories and remembering. Plan what you will write and how you will share your writing.

THEME

Treasures from the Past

Sometimes the past holds hidden treasures that have been forgotten over the years. The selections that follow show how people can unlock the past and its secrets.

CONTENTS

SUNKEN TREASURE
by Gail Gibbons

CHILDREN'S CHOICE

"It's there! It's really there!"

The rotting hull of a ship has been found on the ocean floor. Within the wreck lies a fabulous treasure. The story of each underwater treasure hunt is different, but each goes back to the same beginning . . . the sinking of a ship. The story of the hunt for the *Nuestra Señora de Atocha,* a Spanish galleon, begins the same way.

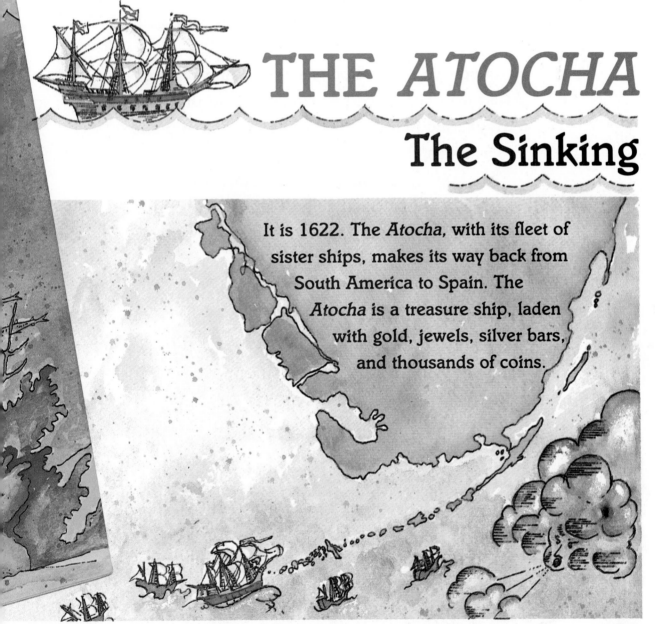

THE *ATOCHA*
The Sinking

It is 1622. The *Atocha,* with its fleet of sister ships, makes its way back from South America to Spain. The *Atocha* is a treasure ship, laden with gold, jewels, silver bars, and thousands of coins.

The fleet makes a stop in Cuba and then sets off again. As the ships near Florida, a hurricane gathers strength.

Wind rips at the *Atocha*'s sails. Spray washes across the deck. The 265 people aboard the ship are terrified. Suddenly, a huge wave lifts the ship and throws it against a reef.

The hull breaks open, and the *Atocha*—along with several of its sister ships—sinks beneath the waves. All but five aboard the *Atocha* drown.

The Search

Spain wants its treasure back. Search ships are sent out. They find one of the *Atocha*'s sister ships, the *Santa Margarita*, and salvage begins. Sponge and pearl divers bring some of the *Santa Margarita*'s treasure to the surface.

But the *Atocha* cannot be found.

Hundreds of years go by. The *Atocha* is almost forgotten. Storms and strong sea currents scatter its treasure for miles along the ocean floor. The ship slowly rots and breaks into pieces. Sand covers the remains.

In the early 1960's, a new search begins. A man named Mel Fisher has read about the *Atocha*. He is determined to find the lost treasure ship. He will need boats, crew, and equipment. Investors provide the money, and the venture gets under way.

Search boats go to where it is believed the *Atocha* went down.

The boats are fitted with modern equipment for exploring the ocean bottom.

mailboxes

When the instruments register a "hit," divers go down to investigate. They keep in view of each other and regularly check their air supplies.

Large elbow-shaped pipes, called mailboxes, are swung into place. The mailboxes are Mel Fisher's invention. The whirling of the boat's propellers forces water through the mailboxes, blowing large holes in the sand. If anything is buried, it will be uncovered.

But only litter is found—nothing of value, nothing from the *Atocha*.

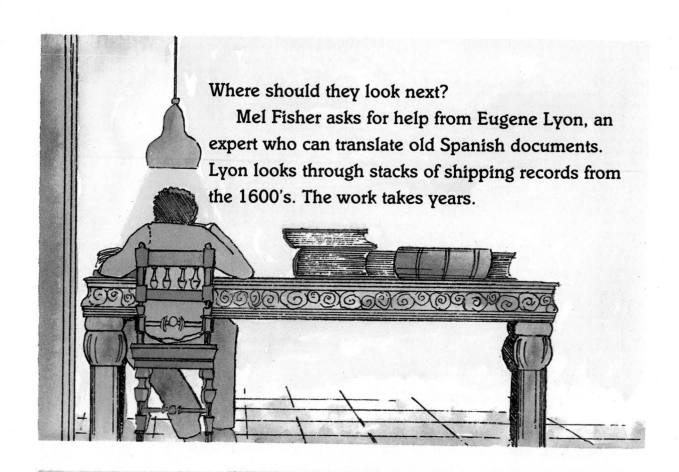

Where should they look next?

Mel Fisher asks for help from Eugene Lyon, an expert who can translate old Spanish documents. Lyon looks through stacks of shipping records from the 1600's. The work takes years.

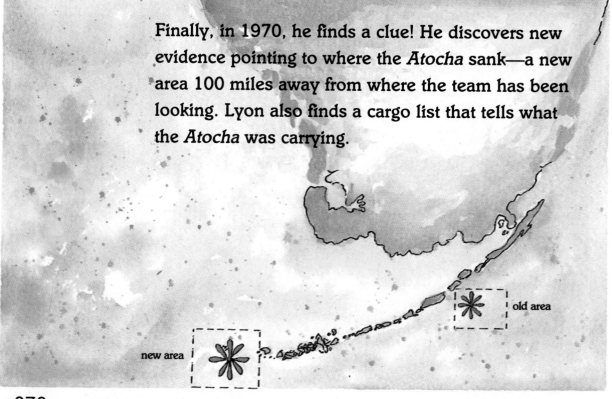

Finally, in 1970, he finds a clue! He discovers new evidence pointing to where the *Atocha* sank—a new area 100 miles away from where the team has been looking. Lyon also finds a cargo list that tells what the *Atocha* was carrying.

old area

new area

A search boat moves to the new location.

In 1971, a huge galleon anchor, several muskets, and gold bars and chains are found. But are they from the *Atocha*? There is no way to prove it.

Two years later, three heavy silver bars are recovered. The bars with their markings match up with the *Atocha*'s cargo list. Now they have proof!

Then, in 1975, the *Atocha's* bronze cannons are found. The crew believe they are getting closer to the mother lode . . . the main treasure of the ship.

But they are wrong. Day after day they search the huge area. Many more years go by. Crew members leave and new ones sign on. When the money runs out, new investors must be found.

The Find

1985. The crew go back and search a site they had searched years ago. And then it happens—a big "hit" registers on their equipment. Divers go down.

"We found it! The mother lode!"

Mel Fisher's twenty-year search is finally over. Resting on the ocean floor, 55 feet below, is the *Atocha*'s fabled treasure—glinting gold bars, jewelry, gold and silver coins, and other precious finds. Nearly all the listed cargo is there, and more—some treasure must have been smuggled aboard.

The Recording

The crew works with a marine archaeologist, Duncan Mathewson. He insists that the mother lode not be disturbed. A grid of plastic pipes is laid over the site.

underwater camera

The divers take pictures and make drawings square by square. Each square of the grid is numbered. That way the exact position of each timber, coin, and artifact is recorded.

Later, archaeologists and historians will use this information to learn about times past.

underwater slate

grid marker number

The Salvage

Now the treasure can be brought to the surface.
Salvage boats are moved in. Divers descend and crew
members lower baskets over the side to them.

The divers gently fan the sand with their hands
and use an airlift to carefully suck it away.

airlift

As treasure is recovered, other artifacts are exposed underneath. Each piece of treasure must be accounted for. Again, everything found is sketched and photographed.

One after another, baskets full of treasure are raised to the surface.

Each day the work continues . . . dive after dive after dive. More treasure is recovered from the deep. It is hard work and can be done only in good weather.

The salvage goes on for weeks, months, and years.

Restoration and Preservation

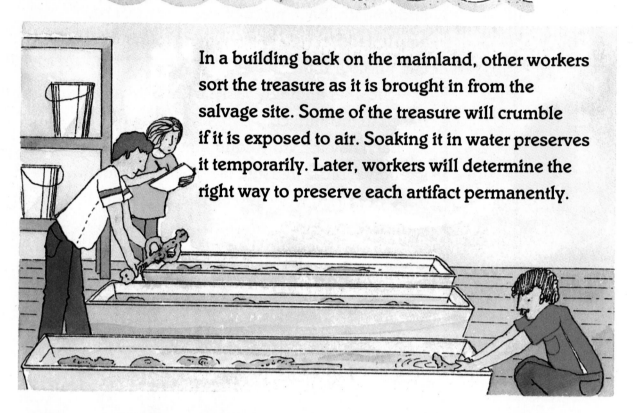

In a building back on the mainland, other workers sort the treasure as it is brought in from the salvage site. Some of the treasure will crumble if it is exposed to air. Soaking it in water preserves it temporarily. Later, workers will determine the right way to preserve each artifact permanently.

Silver coins are put into chemical baths to clean and restore them. In one or two days they will look like new.

Silver bars soak in chemical baths, too, but they will take longer to clean. They are bigger. The gold from the *Atocha* is already shiny— gold never loses its luster.

There were many pottery storage jars on board the *Atocha*. Amazingly, some are recovered whole. Other jars had been shattered and now must be pieced together again.

Cataloging

Cataloging of the *Atocha's* treasure is done in several ways:

A photographer takes pictures of a sword.

Coins are scanned by a computer, and an exact description of each one is stored in the computer's memory.

An artist draws pictures of a gold plate and an emerald-studded necklace.

This kind of careful cataloging provides a valuable record for the future.

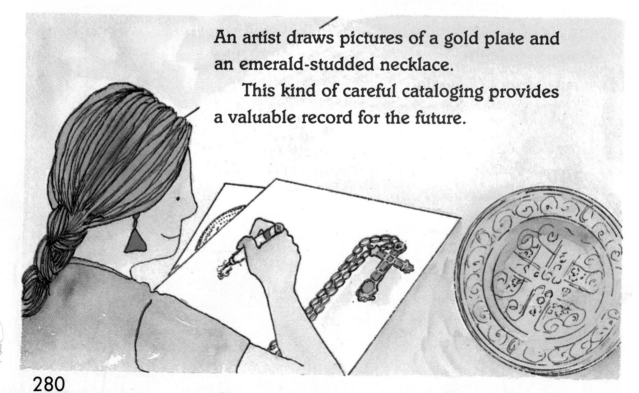

Distribution

Some of the treasure will go to museums.

Some will go to the investors and some will go to the crew. All of them made it possible for Mel Fisher's long search to continue. A computer works out what each one's fair share will be.

The treasure of the *Nuestra Señora de Atocha* is valued at hundreds of millions of dollars . . . a very wealthy treasure ship indeed!

The wreck and its artifacts will be studied by historians and archaeologists for years to come. Their discoveries will enrich our knowledge of the past. This will be the second treasure of the *Atocha*.

ANOTHER FAMOUS TREASURE HUNT
THE MARY ROSE • an English warship

The Sinking

In 1545, the *Mary Rose*, the pride of Henry VIII's fleet, set sail to do battle against the French. She never fired a shot. Overloaded with guns and armed men, she sank off the coast of England.

The Search

In 1965, a group of British historians undertook a search for the *Mary Rose*. They knew approximately where she had gone down, but over the centuries she had been buried in sand and silt.

The Find

Two years later the *Mary Rose* was found.

The Salvage

For years divers salvaged at the site. Then, in 1982, modern equipment was used to raise the hull of the ship.

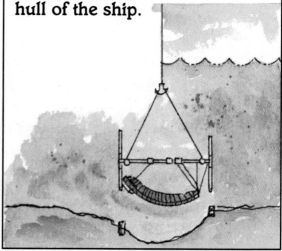

Restoration & Preservation

A special museum was built to house the hull of the *Mary Rose*. The hull must be constantly sprayed with a cold-water mist to keep the wood from disintegrating. Eventually, a waxy preserving solution will be added to the mist. The process of preservation will be completed in 2001.

Learning About the Past

The layers of mud that had settled on the *Mary Rose* preserved fragile pieces of clothing, shoes and boots. From these we know what sailors wore in 16th-century England.

By studying the hull, historians learned about shipbuilding methods at that time.

Would you want to be a member of Mel Fisher's crew? Why or why not?

What probably happened to the *Atocha*?

Mel Fisher's search took many years. Why do you think some people gave up the search, while Mel and other members of the crew never did?

WRITE   Finding something that has been lost is not always easy. Make a list of steps that you would take to find something. Write the steps in order.

Author AND Illustrator:

GAIL GIBBONS

AWARD-WINNING
AUTHOR AND
ILLUSTRATOR

One morning I got a call from a woman named Chris Paterson. She was a friend of the archaeologist who had been searching for the *Atocha*. The treasure had been found only a few days earlier, but the search had been going on for years. "Why don't you write a book about sunken treasure?" she asked. I thought it was an exciting idea, so I called my editor, who said, "Let's do it right now."

My husband, Kent, and I went to Key West, Florida, three times. We toured the building where the treasure from the *Atocha* was being processed. I was right there as it was being lifted out of the ocean. The most amazing thing I saw really wasn't the treasure as much as the excitement and dedication of the people who found it.

What also fascinated me was the restoration process. There were people in the back of the building piecing pottery together and polishing up other pieces of the treasure. The work was highly organized, but no one knew what the divers would be bringing up next.

This mariner's astrolabe was recovered from the *Atocha* wreck site.

Mailboxes are used to move sand on the bottom of the ocean to uncover wrecks and treasure.

I was very taken with the history of it all. For instance, one thing the divers recovered was an astrolabe, a measuring device once used in navigation. That was the kind of "treasure" that interested me the most.

At the treasure site, my husband took photographs while I asked questions. Then I drew the pictures in the book from Kent's photos. When I started *Sunken Treasure*, there was very little information on the *Atocha* search, so much of my research is original. Whenever you write nonfiction, you have to cross-check your facts. You can't just rely on information you find in other books. That's why I like to go to the source myself.

Mel Fisher has found his treasure.

I started this kind of writing because my editor wanted more exciting nonfiction. So I wrote a book called *Clocks and How They Go,* and I found out I really liked the research part of writing. The most exciting part of nonfiction for me is taking complicated subjects and making them easy to understand. The hardest thing to make clear in *Sunken Treasure* was the gridwork process used to record the position of each piece of the treasure. Another tough part was finding pictures of past events, such as the loading of the *Atocha,* so I could re-create them as illustrations.

Gail Gibbons holds a massive gold chain recovered from the wreck of the Atocha.

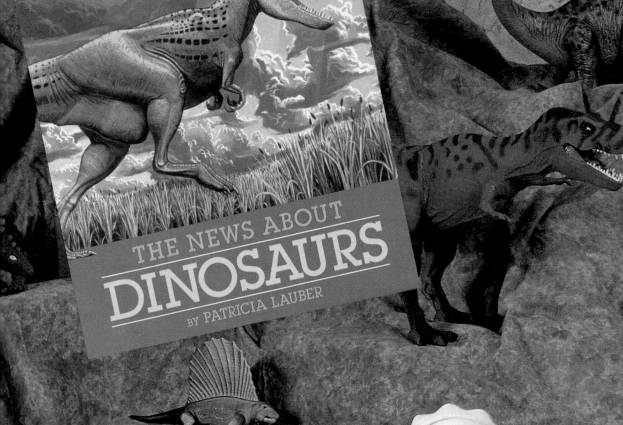

THE NEWS ABOUT
DINOSAURS

BY PATRICIA LAUBER

OUTSTANDING
SCIENCE TRADE
BOOK

SLJ BEST BOOKS
OF THE YEAR

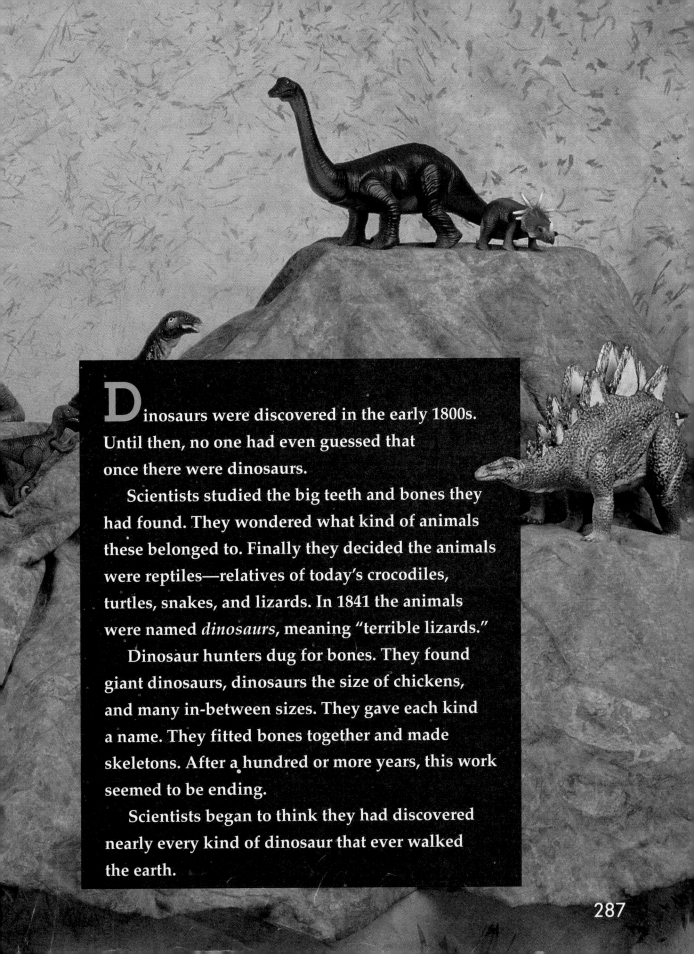

Dinosaurs were discovered in the early 1800s. Until then, no one had even guessed that once there were dinosaurs.

Scientists studied the big teeth and bones they had found. They wondered what kind of animals these belonged to. Finally they decided the animals were reptiles—relatives of today's crocodiles, turtles, snakes, and lizards. In 1841 the animals were named *dinosaurs*, meaning "terrible lizards."

Dinosaur hunters dug for bones. They found giant dinosaurs, dinosaurs the size of chickens, and many in-between sizes. They gave each kind a name. They fitted bones together and made skeletons. After a hundred or more years, this work seemed to be ending.

Scientists began to think they had discovered nearly every kind of dinosaur that ever walked the earth.

THE NEWS IS:

The work was far from finished. Today new kinds of dinosaurs are found all the time. And scientists think there must be hundreds more that they haven't discovered yet. Four of the new kinds they have found are *Baryonyx* (BAR-ee-ON-ix), *Mamenchisaurus* (mah-MEN-chee-sawr-us), *Deinonychus* (dyne-ON-ik-us), and *Nanotyrannus* (NAN-o-tie-ran-us).

▼

Baryonyx **was 30 feet long, with 15-inch claws and a snout like a crocodile's. It probably lived along rivers and used its claws and snout to catch fish. It was discovered near London, England, by a plumber whose hobby was searching for fossils, traces of ancient life preserved in rock.** ***Baryonyx*** **means "heavy claw."**

Mamenchisaurus was a giant plant-eating dinosaur, 72 feet long. Its 33-foot neck is the longest of any known animal.

Deinonychus was found in Montana. It was fairly small, about 9 feet long, and walked on its hind legs. Each hind foot had a big claw, shaped like a curved sword.

Nanotyrannus was a small relative of Tyrannosaurus rex. This small meat-eating dinosaur looked like its big relative but was only one-tenth as heavy and one-third as long—it weighed about 1,000 pounds and was 17 feet long.

For many years, people thought of dinosaurs as slow-moving and slow-witted. That is how they appear in this 1870s painting by Benjamin Waterhouse Hawkins. He was the first artist to work closely with scientists who were studying dinosaurs.

Most reptiles walk with their knees bent and their feet wide apart. Scientists used to think dinosaurs must have walked the same way. They pictured dinosaurs as slow and clumsy, waddling along with their tails dragging on the ground. So that was how dinosaurs were made to look in books and museums.

THE NEWS IS:

Dinosaurs didn't look like that at all. They were good walkers. They held their tails up. And many kinds were quick and nimble. Today's scientists have learned this by studying dinosaur footprints.

When dinosaurs walked in mud or wet sand, they left footprints. Most of these tracks washed or oozed away. But in some places the tracks hardened. Later they were buried under mud or sand that turned to rock. The tracks were preserved in the rock—they became fossils.

▼

Today dinosaurs are shown as lively and active. These huge, horned plant-eaters are driving off *Albertosaurus* (al-BER-tuh-sawr-us), a fierce meat-eater.

Camarasaurs (KAM-uh-ruh-saurz), in the foreground, and *camptosaurs* (KAMP-tuh-sawrz) are crossing a recently flooded area and leaving footprints. Preserved in rock, such tracks have revealed much about dinosaurs.

Tracks show that dinosaurs walked in long, easy strides. Their legs and feet were under their bodies, not out to the side. Their bodies were high off the ground. Big plant-eaters walked at 3 or 4 miles an hour. Some small meat-eaters could run as fast as 35 or 40 miles an hour.

Which one of the four new dinosaurs do you find the most interesting? Give reasons for your answer.

Why do you think people like to read the "news" about dinosaurs?

WRITE Choose a favorite dinosaur. Find out more about it, and write three sentences that tell how it looked, what it ate, and what probably happened to it.

Treasures from the Past

How is searching for dinosaurs like searching for sunken treasure? Which kind of search would you enjoy more? Why?

WRITER'S WORKSHOP

Think of several questions about the past that you would like to have answered. Choose one question. Then go to the library to find the answer. Organize your information, and write a report to share what you learn.

Writer's Choice: You might want to write about something that is *not* from the past. Find out what you can about your topic. Choose an original way to share your information.

T H E M E

Was It Real?

Some of the adventures you have may be more exciting than others, but they are all real adventures. As you read the following stories, you may have to think carefully to decide whether the adventures are real or imaginary.

C O N T E N T S

The Wreck of the Zephyr

The Wreck of the Zephyr

CHRIS VAN ALLSBURG

ALA NOTABLE
BOOK
CHILDREN'S CHOICE
NEW YORK TIMES
BEST ILLUSTRATED
BOOKS OF THE
YEAR

Company

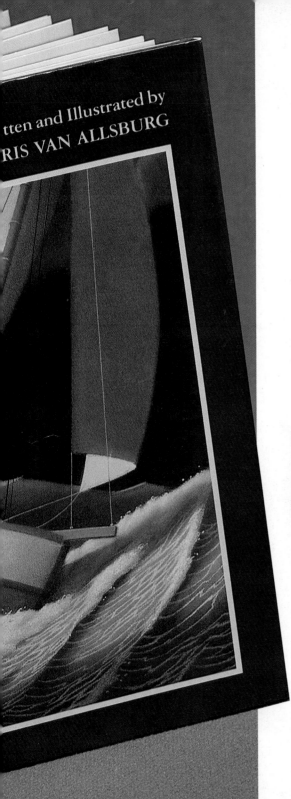

Once, while traveling along the seashore, I stopped at a small fishing village. After eating lunch, I decided to take a walk. I followed a path out of the village, uphill to some cliffs high above the sea. At the edge of these cliffs was a most unusual sight—the wreck of a small sailboat.

An old man was sitting among the broken timbers, smoking a pipe. He seemed to be reading my mind when he said, "Odd, isn't it?"

"Yes," I answered. "How did it get here?"

"Waves carried it up during a storm."

"Really?" I said. "It doesn't seem the waves could ever get that high."

Written and Illustrated by
CHRIS VAN ALLSBURG

The old man smiled. "Well, there is another story." He invited me to have a seat and listen to his strange tale.

"In our village, years ago," he said, "there was a boy who could sail a boat better than any man in the harbor. He could find a breeze over the flattest sea. When dark clouds kept other boats at anchor, the boy would sail out, ready to prove to the villagers, to the sea itself, how great a sailor he was.

"One morning, under an ominous sky, he prepared to take his boat, the *Zephyr*, out to sea. A fisherman warned the boy to stay in port. Already a strong wind was blowing. 'I'm not afraid,' the boy said, 'because I'm the greatest sailor there is.' The fisherman pointed to a sea gull gliding overhead. 'There's the only sailor who can go out on a day like this.' The boy just laughed as he hoisted his sails into a blustery wind.

"The wind whistled in the rigging as the *Zephyr* pounded her way through the water. The sky grew black and the waves rose up like mountains. The boy struggled to keep his boat from going over. Suddenly a gust of wind caught the sail. The boom swung around and hit the boy's head. He fell to the cockpit floor and did not move.

"When the boy opened his eyes, he found himself lying on a beach. The *Zephyr* rested behind him, carried there by the storm. The boat was far from the water's edge. The tide would not carry it back to sea. The boy set out to look for help.

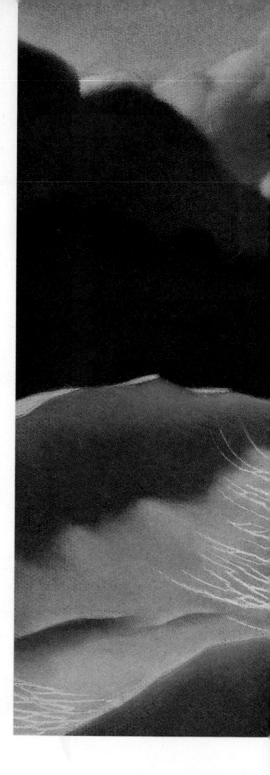

"He walked for a long time and was surprised that he didn't recognize the shoreline. He climbed a hill, expecting to see something familiar, but what he saw instead was a strange and unbelievable sight. Before him were two boats, sailing high above the water. Astonished, he watched them glide by. Then a third sailed past, towing the *Zephyr.* The boats entered a bay that was bordered by a large village. There they left the *Zephyr.*

"The boy made his way down to the
harbor, to the dock where his boat was
tied. He met a sailor who smiled when he
saw the boy. Pointing to the *Zephyr* he
asked, 'Yours?' The boy nodded. The
sailor said they almost never saw strangers
on their island. It was surrounded by a
treacherous reef. The *Zephyr* must have
been carried over the reef by the storm. He
told the boy that, later, they would take
him and the *Zephyr* back over the reef.
But the boy said he would not leave until
he learned to sail above the waves. The
sailor told him it took years to learn to sail
like that. 'Besides,' he said, 'the *Zephyr*
does not have the right sails.' The boy
insisted. He pleaded with the sailor.

"Finally the sailor said he would try to teach him if the boy promised to leave the next morning. The boy agreed. The sailor went to a shed and got a new set of sails.

"All afternoon they sailed back and forth across the bay. Sometimes the sailor took the tiller, and the boat would magically begin to lift out of the water. But when the boy tried, he could not catch the wind that made boats fly.

"When the sun went down they went back to the harbor. They dropped anchor and a fisherman rowed them to shore. 'In the morning,' the sailor said, 'we'll put your own sails back on the *Zephyr* and send you home.' He took the boy to his house, and the sailor's wife fed them oyster stew.

"After dinner the sailor played the concertina. He sang a song about a man named Samuel Blue, who, long ago, tried to sail his boat over land and crashed:

'For the wind o'er land's ne'er steady nor true,

an' all men that sail there'll meet Samuel Blue.'

"When he was done with his song, the sailor sent the boy to bed. But the boy could not sleep. He knew he could fly his boat if he had another chance. He waited until the sailor and his wife were asleep, then he quietly dressed and went to the harbor. As he rowed out to the *Zephyr,* the boy felt the light evening wind grow stronger and colder.

"Under a full moon, he sailed the *Zephyr* into the bay. He tried to remember everything the sailor had told him. He tried to feel the wind pulling his boat forward, lifting it up. Then, suddenly, the boy felt the *Zephyr* begin to shake. The sound of the water rushing past the hull grew louder. The air filled with spray as the boat sliced through the waves. The bow slowly began to lift. Higher and higher the *Zephyr* rose out of the water, then finally broke free. The sound of rushing water stopped. There was only the sound of wind in the sails. The *Zephyr* was flying.

"Using the stars to guide him, the boy set a course for home. The wind blew very hard, churning the sea below. But that did not matter to the *Zephyr* as she glided through the night sky. When clouds blocked the boy's view of the stars, he trimmed the sails and climbed higher. Surely the men of the island never dared fly so high. Now the boy was certain he was truly the greatest sailor of all.

"He steered well. Before the night was over, he saw the moonlit spire of the church at the edge of his village. As he drew closer to land, an idea took hold of him. He would sail over the village and ring the *Zephyr*'s bell. Then everyone would see him and know that he was the greatest sailor. He flew over the tree-topped cliffs of the shore, but as he reached the church the *Zephyr* began to fall.

"The wind had shifted. The boy pulled as hard as he could on the tiller, but it did no good. The wind shifted again. He steered for the open sea, but the trees at the cliff's edge stood between him and the water. At first there was just the rustle of leaves brushing the hull. Then the air was filled with the sound of breaking branches and ripping sails. The boat fell to the ground. And here she sits today."

"A remarkable tale," I said, as the old man stopped to relight his pipe. "What happened to the boy?"

"He broke his leg that night. Of course, no one believed his story about flying boats. It was easier for them to believe that he was lost in the storm and thrown up here by the waves." The old man laughed.

"No sir, the boy never amounted to much. People thought he was crazy. He just took odd jobs around the harbor. Most of the time he was out sailing, searching for that island and a new set of sails."

A light breeze blew through the trees. The old man looked up. "Wind coming," he said, "I've got some sailing to do." He picked up a cane, and I watched as he limped slowly toward the harbor.

Think about the boy who tried to fly the *Zephyr.* How would you describe his personality?

Which parts of this story seem real? Which parts seem unreal?

If you could ask the man telling the story one question, what would it be?

WRITE   Write a poem that tells how it would feel to fly a sailboat.

WORDS ABOUT THE

AUTHOR
AND
ILLUSTRATOR:

CHRIS VAN ALLSBURG

Chris Van Allsburg liked to draw when he was a boy, especially cartoon characters such as Dagwood Bumstead. But it wasn't until he went to college that he began to study art seriously. First he was a sculptor, but a friend who illustrated children's books suggested he try his hand at drawing for books, too. Van Allsburg's wife was a teacher, and she brought home books for him to look at. Then he tried one of his own. To his surprise, it was successful! Since that first book, published in 1979, Van Allsburg has become one of the most popular authors writing and drawing for young people.

Although Van Allsburg had written and illustrated two picture books before *The Wreck of the Zephyr*, this was the first book he did in color. The others had only black-and-white drawings. "Working in color is far more difficult," he says.

"When you draw in black and white, you only have to worry about how dark something is, but when there are so many different colors you can use, there's a lot more to think about. I started to work in color because it was something different and interesting."

Van Allsburg wrote *The Wreck of the Zephyr* because he wanted to do a story that took place outdoors. When he was younger, he spent a good deal of time sailing on Lake Michigan. Maybe because of that, he had a picture in his mind of a flying boat, though he says, "I'm really not sure where that image came from." After he drew the picture of the boat flying past a lighthouse, he decided to find the story behind it. Van Allsburg says *The Wreck of the Zephyr* is about possibilities—you can't be too sure what will happen in life.

Once he gets the idea for a book, it takes Van Allsburg about five months to draw the pictures and write the story. "I'm slow," he says. "I know people who make art much faster than I do. I make sketches and doodles on pieces of paper. I write story outlines. I work on what I think is the strongest idea I have at the time. I keep all the other ideas. Not in a sketchbook, though. Right now, I've got about 200 ideas floating around in my head."

Why Can't I Fly?

written and illustrated by Ken Brown

Early one morning, all the animals were gathered, as usual, by the water.

"I wish I could fly," thought the Ostrich. "Why can't I fly?" he asked the Sparrow.

"Maybe your neck is too long," suggested the Sparrow.

"The flamingoes have long necks and they can fly," replied the Ostrich, "so why can't I?"

"I don't know," chirped the Sparrow, "perhaps your legs are too long."

"The storks have long legs and they can fly," said the Ostrich, "so why can't I?"

"Well, perhaps your wings are too small," said the Sparrow.

"You've got small wings and you can fly," answered the Ostrich, "so why can't I?"

"Well, I don't know! Maybe you just don't try hard enough," and so saying, the Sparrow flew away.

"Try hard enough indeed!" thought the Ostrich. "I'll show him. I'll show all of them that I can fly." So he ran as fast as he could and, flapping his wings, he jumped off a high sand dune . . . only to land, seconds later, with a terrible thud.

Next he climbed to the top of a huge rock.

"I'll show them!" he panted.

With his wings flailing the air, he threw himself over the edge, but instantly plunged downward and landed headfirst in the soft sand below.

He remained with his head in the sand, too embarrassed to show his face.

"I'll show them!" he thought. "If my wings are too small, I'll make them bigger."

Using some large leaves, bamboo canes, strong vines, and a great deal of skill, he constructed a flying machine.

Then he climbed to the top of the high rock again, and launched himself into the air.

"This is it! Look at me, everyone. I'm flying," cried the Ostrich.

But he spoke too soon! Moments later, he landed with an almighty splash right in the middle of the river.

"Never mind," said the Sparrow. "Your long neck will keep your head well above water!"

But the Ostrich was not put off by this, his first disastrous attempt at flying. He built another flying machine with even bigger wings and once again launched himself into the air.

"Out of my way!" he shouted to the doves. "Out of my way—I'm flying!"

Alas, this flight also ended in complete disaster, when the Ostrich became totally entangled in the leaves of a high palm tree.

"Never mind!" chirped the Sparrow. "Your long legs will certainly help you to get down from there."

The Ostrich, however, was just as determined as ever to fly; he would not give up. So he built an even bigger flying machine and for the third time climbed to the top of the high rock. He took a deep breath and launched himself yet again into the air. This time, instead of plummeting straight downward as before, he soared high up into the sky, as gracefully as any other bird. "Look at me!" shouted the triumphant Ostrich. "Look, everybody, I'm flying!"

But the only reply that he got was the sound of his own voice echoing about the empty skies.

The Ostrich couldn't understand it!

"Where is everyone?" he cried. "Where's Sparrow? I'm flying and there's no one here to see. They'll never believe me now."

But they did!

The Ostrich wishes he could fly. What do you wish you could do? Name some things you could do to reach your goal.

If you wanted to tell someone, in just a few words, what this story is like, what would you say?

WRITE Suppose you have a friend who is trying something new. Write a paragraph in which you give a friend helpful advice so that he or she won't give up.

Was It Real?

Sometimes what happens in a story seems a little bit real, even when you know it is not. Sometimes a story is just plain silly. Which of the stories you just read seems more real? Which one seems sillier? Tell why you feel as you do.

WRITER'S WORKSHOP

If Ostrich and the boy in "The Wreck of the *Zephyr*" met, what would they say to each other? Write some dialogue, or speaking parts, for Ostrich and the boy. You can make your dialogue seem real or silly.

Writer's Choice:
You might want to write something else about the stories you have read. Decide what you will write, and plan how you will share your work.

CONNECTIONS

Multicultural Connection

Our Nation Remembers

What building in your town contains more portraits of famous Americans than a museum or a library? The answer is— the post office!

The United States Postal Service prints new stamps several times each year. Many of these stamps honor the memories of great Americans.

These Americans have left their marks on our nation's history. Matthew A. Henson was a great explorer. Ida B. Wells was a newspaper writer, editor, and owner. Do you recognize the other people shown?

Do research to find out what is special about one of these people. Share what you learn with your classmates. You may want to use the facts to make a bulletin board display.

Social Studies Connection

Memories All Around

Does your community remember its special people by naming places after them? Find out the stories behind a few of the names. Then make a guidebook that shows these places and tells about them.

Art Connection

Stamped in Your Memory

Draw a design for a United States stamp that shows an American you admire. Write a caption that tells why this person should be remembered. Display your work on a bulletin board.

GLOSSARY

The **pronunciation** of each word in this glossary is shown by a phonetic respelling in brackets; for example, [ə•kā′zhən•əl•ē]. An accent mark (′) follows the syllable with the most stress: [kun′ing]. A secondary, or lighter, accent mark (′) follows a syllable with less stress: [par′ə•sho͞ot′]. The key to other pronunciation symbols is below. You will find a shortened version of this key on alternate pages of the glossary.

a	add, map	m	move, seem	u	up, done
ā	ace, rate	n	nice, tin	û(r)	burn, term
â(r)	care, air	ng	ring, song	yo͞o	fuse, few
ä	palm, father	o	odd, hot	v	vain, eve
b	bat, rub	ō	open, so	w	win, away
ch	check, catch	ô	order, jaw	y	yet, yearn
d	dog, rod	oi	oil, boy	z	zest, muse
e	end, pet	ou	pout, now	zh	vision, pleasure
ē	equal, tree	o͝o	took, full	ə	the schwa,
f	fit, half	o͞o	pool, food		an unstressed
g	go, log	p	pit, stop		vowel representing
h	hope, hate	r	run, poor		the sound spelled
i	it, give	s	see, pass		a in *above*
ī	ice, write	sh	sure, rush		e in *sicken*
j	joy, ledge	t	talk, sit		i in *possible*
k	cool, take	th	thin, both		o in *melon*
l	look, rule	~~th~~	this, bathe		u in *circus*

Pronunciation Key*

*Adapted entries, the Pronunciation Key, and the Short Key that appear on the following pages are reprinted from *HBJ School Dictionary*. Copyright © 1990 by Harcourt Brace & Company. Reprinted by permission of Harcourt Brace & Company.

A

acacia

a·board [ə·bôrd'] *prep.*
On, in, or into: **Everyone**
aboard **the plane**
enjoyed seeing
wonderful views of the
Grand Canyon.

a·ca·cia [ə·kā'shə] *n.* A
tree with yellow or
white flowers, found in
warm areas: **All the**
acacia **trees died during**
the rare cold spell.

acre *Acre* is from the
Latin word *ager* and the
Greek word *agros* meaning
"field." As early as A.D.
1000, *acre* referred to a
measured area of land,
specifically the amount of
land a pair of oxen could
plow in one day.

a·cre [ā'kər] *n.* An area of
land that is as big as a
square with sides about
210 feet long: **One**
square mile is 640 *acres.*

a·gent [ā'jənt] *n.* A person
who acts with
instructions from
someone else; a person
who represents a group:
The FBI *agent* **spent a**
month following and
watching the spy.

anchor

an·chor [ang'kər] *n.* A
heavy piece of metal
tied to a boat and
dropped into the water
to keep the boat from
moving: **The sailor**
forgot to throw the
anchor **over the side.**

ar·chae·ol·o·gist
[är'kē·ol'ə·jist] *n.* An
expert in the study of
past times and ancient
cultures, mainly through
digging up remains: **The**
archaeologist **was**
interested in finding
buried treasure.

arch·er fish [är'chər fish]
n. A small fish that
catches insects by
stunning them with
drops of water it squirts
from its mouth.

ar·ti·fact [är'tə·fakt'] *n.*
Something made by
humans: **The most**
interesting *artifact* **the**
explorer found was a
carved wooden box.

at·tic [at'ik] *n.* The top
floor of a house, right
under the roof: **The**
twins liked to play in
the *attic* **so they could**
hear the squirrels
running across the roof.

at·tract [ə·trakt'] *v.*
at·tract·ed, at·tract·ing
To grab the attention of
someone or something;
to cause someone or
something to come near:
The baby was *attracted*
to my silver bracelet.

332

awl [ôl] *n.* A pointed tool used to punch holes in wood or leather: **My grandfather used an** *awl* **to make holes in my new leather belt.**

B

back•ing [bak'ing] *n.* Something attached to a fabric for extra strength and support: **The bathroom rug has a rubber** *backing.*

bac•te•ria [bak•tir'ē•ə] *n. pl.* One-celled living things too small to be seen without a microscope: **Although** *bacteria* **are small, some can cause diseases.**

bam•boo [bam•bōo'] *adj.* Made of a tall grass with hard, hollow stems: **All the furniture in the house was made of oak except for the beautiful** *bamboo* **table in front of the sofa.**

ban•dit [ban'dit] *n.* A robber: **The** *bandit* **opened the gate and stole the fastest horses from the king's stables.**

bar•ri•er [bar'ē•ər] *n.* Something blocking the way: **The fat little puppy tried to climb over the** *barrier* **at the door so it could get out of the kitchen.**

bed•roll [bed'rōl] *n.* A sleeping bag or a thin mattress that is rolled up: **Tran always brought an extra blanket to use with his** *bedroll* **so he would be warm when he slept.**

be•lat•ed [bi•lā'tid] *adj.* Too late: **Amy's** *belated* **birthday card arrived in the mail six days after Jan's birthday.**

be•yond [bi•yond'] *prep.* At a distance farther away: **The new mall is being built just** *beyond* **his house.**

blus•ter•y [blus'tər•ē] *adj.* Blowing strongly: **The cold,** *blustery* **wind blew snow on us.**

bo•a [bō'ə] *n.* A long scarf made of feathers or fur: **Ms. Brown liked to wear her feather** *boa* **around her neck.**

bamboo

bandit A *bandit* meant someone who was sent away or "banished." It came from the Italian word *bandito,* which was connected to a word meaning "to ban."

a	add	o͝o	took
ā	ace	o͞o	pool
â	care	u	up
ä	palm	û	burn
e	end	yo͞o	fuse
ē	equal	oi	oil
i	it	ou	pout
ī	ice	ng	ring
o	odd	th	thin
ō	open	th	this
ô	order	zh	vision

ə = { a in *above* e in *sicken*
        i in *possible*
        o in *melon* u in *circus* }

bolt [bōlt] *n.* A metal screw or pin used with a nut to hold something in place: **Kim used two small *bolts* to fasten the bell to his bicycle.**

bore [bôr] *v.* **bored, bor•ing** To make someone feel uninterested and tired of something: **The movie *bored* the children.**

bounce [bouns] *v.* **bounced, bounc•ing** To spring back from a surface, after touching it; to jump: **Ray's hand *bounced* off the punching bag.**

bow

bow [bō] *n.* A curved piece of wood used with a string to shoot arrows: **Even though her *bow* broke after she shot the arrow, Ellen was able to hit the target.**

bowl•er [bō′lər] *n.* A round, hard hat made of felt: **Dwayne sat on his grandfather's *bowler*, squashing it so Grandpa couldn't wear it anymore.**

bowler

brit•tle [brit′(ə)l] *adj.* Easily broken or snapped: **The candy**

was so *brittle* it broke.

browse [brouz] *v.* To feed on grass, leaves, and twigs: **The cows, sheep, and horses *browse* quietly in the fields every afternoon in the summer.** *syn.* graze

C

can•yon [kan′yən] *n.* A very deep area between hills or mountains: **The color of the rock in the *canyons* is quite breathtaking.**

car•go [kär′gō] *n.* The goods carried by a boat or a plane: **They unloaded the *cargo* of bananas and coffee from the hold of the ship from South America.**

cat•a•log [kat′ə•lôg′ *or* kat′ə•log′] *v.* **cat•a•loged, cat•a•log•ing** To make a list of names and objects with a description of each one: **The librarian is *cataloging* the library's new books each month.**

ce•dar [sē′dər] *adj.* Made of the reddish wood of a large evergreen tree: **Mrs. Kane made a** *cedar* **chest to keep all her woolen blankets in.**

chauf•feur [shō′fər *or* shō•fûr′] *n.* Someone paid to drive a car: **Mr. Gordon hired a** *chauffeur* **to drive his car so he could work on the way to his office.**

chuck•le [chuk′əl] *v.* To laugh softly: **Andrew began to** *chuckle* **when he saw an** *A* **on his report card.**

churn [chûrn] *v.* **churned, churn•ing** To move about with force: **The motor was** *churning* **the water into white foam behind the boat.**

clam•or [klam′ər] *n.* A loud, steady noise: **The animals in the zoo made such a** *clamor* **at feeding time that people could not hear each other talk.**

clear•ing [klir′ing] *n.* A small area without trees in a forest: **The campers slept soundly in a small** *clearing* **brightened by moonlight.**

cli•ent [klī′ənt] *n.* A customer or a person who uses the professional help of another: **On television shows, a private detective often seems to work for only one** *client.*

cock•pit [kok′pit′] *n.* A low part in a boat where the driver sits: **The Coast Guard officer jumped into the** *cockpit* **and started the motor.**

con•cer•ti•na [kon′sər•tē′nə] *n.* A small musical instrument that is squeezed and pulled apart to make music: **Don played such lively music on his** *concertina* **that we all wanted to dance.**

chauffeur Would you believe that a *chauffeur* once kept a car's engine warm by tending a fire? At one time automobiles were driven by steam engines. One of the driver's jobs was to keep the water in the boiler hot enough to make the steam that powered the car. The word *chauffeur* comes from the French word *chauffer,* which means "to heat."

clearing

concertina

a	add	o͝o	took
ā	ace	o͞o	pool
â	care	u	up
ä	palm	û	burn
e	end	yo͞o	fuse
ē	equal	oi	oil
i	it	ou	pout
ī	ice	ng	ring
o	odd	th	thin
ō	open	t̶h̶	this
ô	order	zh	vision

ə = { a in *above* e in *sicken*
        i in *possible*
        o in *melon* u in *circus*

continent *Continent* comes from the Latin *continens*, meaning "to hold, enclose, or contain," as in self-restraint. It came to be used in combination with the word *terra*. *Terra continens* means "continuous land."

dart

con·gress·man [kong'gris·man] *n., pl.* **congressmen** A member of the United States Congress who is a man: **The** *congressmen* **voted on the bill.**

con·sume [kən·sōōm'] *v.* **con·sumed, con·sum·ing** To destroy completely: **The fire was** *consuming* **the house so quickly that nothing would be left.**

con·ti·nent [kon'tə·nənt] *n.* One of the seven major land areas of the earth; land areas unbroken by major oceans: **Australia is a** *continent.*

co·or·di·nate [kō·ôr'də·nāt'] *v.* **co·or·di·nat·ed, co·or·di·nat·ing** To make the parts of something work together: **Molly carefully** *coordinated* **the plans for the picnic so that everyone brought something.**

corn [kôrn] *n.* A sore that sometimes grows on toes where shoes rub against them.

cous·in [kuz'(ə)n] *n.* The son or daughter of your uncle or aunt: **Even though I have six aunts, I only have one** *cousin.*

cre·ate [krē·āt'] *v.* **cre·at·ed, cre·at·ing** To make: **Latisha** *created* **a farm scene with clay animals.**

cun·ning [kun'ing] *adj.* Clever: **The fox was so** *cunning* **that it was able to escape from its cage.** *syn.* tricky

cy·cle [sī'kəl] *n.* Events that happen in the same order over and over again: **One of the** *cycles* **of nature is that of the seasons—spring, summer, fall, and winter.**

D

dart [därt] *n.* A small weapon like a tiny arrow that can be shot from a gun or thrown by hand: **Suzy's dad showed her how to throw** *darts* **safely so that they would land in the center of the target.**

disc [disk] *n.* A flat circle: **As the plastic *disc* went spinning through the air, the dog leaped and caught it in its jaws.**

dis·guise [dis·gīz'] *v.* **dis·guised, dis·guis·ing** To change the way something or someone looks: **Rachel *disguised* herself so well that no one knew who she was.**

doc·u·ment [dok'yə·mənt] *n.* A written paper that proves something or gives information: **Mrs. Ivan kept in a locked box the *documents* that proved she was an American citizen.**

drought [drout] *n.* A long period without rain: **We need rain to end the *drought* and save the crops.**

E

ea·ger·ly [ē'gər·lē] *adv.* With great interest or excitement: **Paul waited *eagerly* for his turn.**

ech·o [ek'ō] *n.* A sound that repeats as it bounces back from a solid object: **Gabe heard the *echo* of his name after he shouted it into the canyon.**

e·co·sys·tem [ek'ō·sis'təm *or* ēk'ō·sis'təm] *n.* The living things and nonliving surroundings in an area that work together and affect each other: **Cutting down trees can upset the *ecosystem* of a forest so much that it will rain less and many animals will die.**

ee·rie [ir'ē] *adj.* Weird, strange: **An *eerie* noise somewhere in the old house woke Lydia from a sound sleep.**

em·brace [im·brās'] *v.* **em·braced, em·brac·ing** To hug: **Marie *embraced* the dog so hard that it yelped and tried to squirm away from her.**

en·tire [in·tīr'] *adj.* The whole; complete, with no parts missing.

document

drought *Drought* and *dry* both come from the Old English word *dryge*. This makes sense because a *drought* is "a long period of time without rain." Although *drought* ends like *thought*, say it so that it rhymes with *out*.

a	add	o͝o	took
ā	ace	o͞o	pool
â	care	u	up
ä	palm	û	burn
e	end	yo͞o	fuse
ē	equal	oi	oil
i	it	ou	pout
ī	ice	ng	ring
o	odd	th	thin
ō	open	th	this
ô	order	zh	vision

ə = { a in *above* e in *sicken* i in *possible* o in *melon* u in *circus* }

fleet

fossil This word comes from the Latin *fossilis,* meaning "dug up." It comes from the Latin verb *fodere,* which means "to dig." Today the word *fossil* means "a life form of long ago that has been dug up." People who dig for fossils are excavators.

ev•i•dence [ev′ə•dəns] *n.* Proof that something is true or false: **The thief's fingerprints on the glass were clear** *evidence* **that he had been in the house.**

F

fade [fād] *v.* **fad•ed, fad•ing** To lose color; to become less bright: **The orange lampshade had** *faded* **to a dingy yellow.**

fi•na•le [fə•nä′lē] *n.* The last part of a show: **The concert ended with a grand** *finale* **that included beautiful fireworks.**

fish [fish] *v.* **fished, fish•ing** To try to get something from someone: **Although he kept saying that he hadn't played well, we knew Patrick was** *fishing* **for praise.**

fleet [flēt] *n.* A group of ships from the same country or company.

flur•ry [flûr′ē] *v.* **flur•ried, flur•ry•ing** To blow or stir around suddenly: **Mike tried to rake the leaves** *flurrying* **in the wind, but it seemed impossible.**

foot•print [foot′print′] *n.* The mark a foot leaves when it has been in mud or sand: **Tom left his** *footprints* **in the sand while walking along the shore.**

fos•sil [fos′əl] *n.* An animal of long ago whose remains or impression of its remains were saved and hardened: **Insects caught in a tree's sap that hardened millions of years ago became** *fossils.*

fuel [fyoo′əl] *n.* Something that burns easily to create heat or energy: **Mr. Wang used logs and paper as** *fuel* **when he built a fire.**

fun•gus [fung′gəs] *n.* A plant with no leaves or flowers, such as a mushroom.

fur•ry [fûr'ē] *adj.* Covered with hair: **The kitten yawned and curled up beside the *furry* belly of its mother.**

G

gal•le•on [gal'ē•ən] *n.* A large sailing ship of earlier times: **The divers found a sunken *galleon* still loaded with its rich cargo of gold bars, coins, and jewels.**

gar•lic [gär'lik] *n.* A plant like an onion with a strong taste and smell, often used to flavor food: **Bread toasted with butter and *garlic* is often served with a dinner of spaghetti and meatballs.**

ging•ko [ging'kō *or* jing'kō] *n.* A kind of large tree with fan-shaped leaves, found in Asia and the United States: **Her silver earrings were made in the fanlike shape of leaves from a *gingko*.**

glance [glans] *v.* To look quickly.

gust [gust] *n.* A quick rush of wind: **A *gust* of wind suddenly blew her hat off her head.**

H

half-moon [haf'mo͞on'] *adj.* Shaped like an arc or like the moon when only part of it can be seen: **George drew cartoon people with *half-moon* eyes, so they always looked sleepy.**

har•bor [här'bər] *n.* A safe place near the edge of the water, where boats anchor: **In the afternoon, the sailors climbed aboard their ships, which were waiting in the *harbor*.** *syn.* port

hemp [hemp] *adj.* Made from fibers of a plant, used to make rope.

hitch [hich] *v.* **hitched, hitch•ing** To tie something to something else: **The settlers carefully *hitched* the horses to the wagon before they left.**

gingko The *gingko* tree was first planted in the United States about 1780. The name *gingko* is Japanese, because it grew first in Japan, Korea, and China. The gingko is the oldest kind of tree still in existence. It lived through the Ice Age, which destroyed other kinds of trees.

half-moon

harbor

a	add	o͝o	took
ā	ace	o͞o	pool
â	care	u	up
ä	palm	û	burn
e	end	yo͞o	fuse
ē	equal	oi	oil
i	it	ou	pout
ī	ice	ng	ring
o	odd	th	thin
ō	open	<s>th</s>	this
ô	order	zh	vision

ə = { a in *above* e in *sicken*
i in *possible*
o in *melon* u in *circus* }

landscape

hoist [hoist] *v.* **hoist•ed, hoist•ing**   To raise: **The sailor** *hoisted* **our country's flag on our boat.**

hull [hul] *n.* The body of a ship: **The ship's** *hull* **cracked when the storm drove it onto the rocks.**

I

i•de•a [ī•dē'ə] *n.* A thought: **Tammy had a good** *idea* **for what to do at the picnic.**

in•vest•or [in•vest'ər] *n.* Someone who spends money on something that might bring more money later: **Ten** *investors* **paid for building the amusement park.**

L

lad•en [lād'(ə)n] *adj.* Loaded: *Laden* **with books and papers, Carlos could hardly get up the stairs.**

limo

land•scape [land'skāp'] *n.* A view of an area with its natural surroundings, such as the trees, flowers, and type of land: **The** *landscape* **may be pretty in summer, but in winter these mountains are quite dangerous.**

last [last] *v.* To be a part of for a long time: **Diane's friendship with Jerry will** *last* **a long time because they are both interested in the theater.**

latch [lach] *v.* To fasten something shut: **Walter didn't** *latch* **the gate, so the dog pushed it open and ran away.**

lim•o [lim'ō] *n. informal* A limousine or a very large car: **The performers drove to the theater in a shiny black** *limo.*

limp [limp] *adj.* Without stiffness; not firm: **It was hard to turn the** *limp* **pages of the wet newspapers.**

mask

lope [lōp] *v.* **loped, lop·ing** To run with long, slow steps: **As the mule came** *loping* **along the path, Charlie was able to run and catch it.**

lus·ter [lus′tər] *n.* Shine; brightness: **Eric polished the silver to give it** *luster.*

M

ma·neu·ver [mə·n(y)o͞o′vər] *v.* **ma·neu·vered, ma·neu·ver·ing** To move something with skill: **Mrs. Nikos** *maneuvered* **the car around the bicycles and toys in the driveway.**

marsh [märsh] *n.* A low place where the ground is wet and swampy: **You need to wear waterproof boots when you go out to look for birds in the** *marshes* **near the river.** *syns.* swamp, bog

mask [mask] *n.* Something that covers or hides a face or its expressions: **She covered her face with a** *mask* **that matched her costume perfectly.**

mas·ter·piece [mas′tər·pēs′] *n.* A great work: **The "Mona Lisa" is Leonardo da Vinci's** *masterpiece.*

ma·te·ri·al [mə·tir′ē·əl] *n.* The fabric something is made of: **My costume is made of a shiny** *material.*

may·or [mā′ər] *n.* The person in charge of a town: **The** *mayors* **of ten cities met to talk about improving roads between the cities.**

mead·ow [med′ō] *n.* A field where wild grass grows but few trees: **The children tried to play a game of soccer in the** *meadow,* **but they kept losing the ball in the grass.**

meadow

a	add	o͝o	took
ā	ace	o͞o	pool
â	care	u	up
ä	palm	û	burn
e	end	yo͞o	fuse
ē	equal	oi	oil
i	it	ou	pout
ī	ice	ng	ring
o	odd	th	thin
ō	open	th	this
ô	order	zh	vision

ə = { a in *above*   e in *sicken*
       i in *possible*
       o in *melon*   u in *circus* }

341

mushy

nut

mi·grate [mī′grāt′] *v.*
mi·grat·ed,
mi·grat·ing To move
from one area to settle in
another: **Year after year,
the geese had** *migrated*
**south to avoid the cold
winters.**

mush·y [mush′ē] *adj.* Very
soft and easy to squeeze:
**The banana was so ripe
and** *mushy* **that it oozed
from the peel.** *syn.*
squashy

N

ner·vous [nûr′vəs] *adj.*
Very worried and a little
scared: **The thunder and
rain made the children**
nervous **for a while.**

ni·tro·gen [nī′trə·jən] *n.*
A gas that is necessary
for life: **Farmers
sometimes add material
containing** *nitrogen* **to
the soil so plants will
grow better.**

noc·tur·nal [nok·tûr′nəl]
adj. Active at night:
Nocturnal **animals
sleep during the day.**

nour·ish [nûr′ish] *v.*
nour·ished,
nour·ish·ing To feed; to
keep healthy or to make
something grow with
food: **The milk**
nourished **the lost
kittens, helping them to
grow.**

nut [nut] *n.* A small piece
of metal with a hole in
it, used to hold a bolt in
place: *Nuts* **screw onto
the ends of bolts to
hold things together.**

nu·tri·ent [n(y)ōō′trē·ənt]
n. The useful part of
food: **It is healthier to
eat food that has the
right** *nutrients.*

O

oc·ca·sion·al·ly
[ə·kā′zhən·əl·ē] *adv.*
Sometimes; once in a
while: *Occasionally,* **Mr.
Lee showed a movie in
science class.**

of·fi·cial [ə·fish′əl] *n.* A
person who is in charge
of something: **Health**
officials **warned parents
about the measles.**

om•i•nous [om′ə•nəs] *adj.* Looking or sounding as if something bad or scary will happen: **The sky looked black and** *ominous* **before the thunderstorm brought heavy rain.**

owl•ing [oul′ing] *n.* The act of searching for owls: **When we went** *owling* **all we saw were bats.**

P

par•a•chute [par′ə•shōōt′] *v.* **par•a•chut•ed, par•a•chut•ing**   To slow someone's or something's fall toward the ground by using a parachute, which is a large, umbrella-shaped piece of material, attached to the body or object with straps: **When they jump from an airplane,** *parachuting* **soldiers have an idea where they will land.**

par•ka [pär′kə] *n.* A winter coat with a hood: **Gail loved the** *parka* **with the warm wool lining.**

patch•work [pach′wûrk′] *adj.* Made of many pieces of different cloth sewn together in a design: **Sue is making a** *patchwork* **quilt from scraps of fabric.**

pent•house [pent′hous′] *n.* An apartment on the top floor of a building: **From a** *penthouse* **in New York City, you can see the Statue of Liberty.**

pi•an•o [pē•an′ō] *n.* A musical instrument played by hitting its keys with the fingers: **The old** *piano* **was missing some keys, so the player had to skip some notes of the song.**

pierce [pirs] *v.* **pierced, pierc•ing**   To poke through with something pointed: **The sharp tree branch** *pierced* **a hole in the knee of Brett's brand-new jeans.**

pipe [pīp] *v.* **piped, pip•ing** To speak in a high voice: **While the grown-ups were talking about cooking the turkey, Emma** *piped* **up that she smelled something burning.**

parachute   Did you know that there were parachutes before there were airplanes? As early as 1785 people used parachutes to get out of balloons that were in trouble.

parka

piano   The Italian man who made the first piano in 1711 was proud of his invention. The best and most unusual thing about it was that it could be played both *piano e forte*. In Italian this means "soft and loud."

a	add	ŏŏ	took
ā	ace	ōō	pool
â	care	u	up
ä	palm	û	burn
e	end	yōō	fuse
ē	equal	oi	oil
i	it	ou	pout
ī	ice	ng	ring
o	odd	th	thin
ō	open	th	this
ô	order	zh	vision

ə = { a in *above*   e in *sicken*
      i in *possible*
      o in *melon*   u in *circus* }

pizza

plaid

piz·za [pēt'sə] *n.* A baked flat crust covered with cheese, tomato sauce, and other food.

plaid [plad] *n.* A pattern on cloth with stripes of different colors that cross each other: **The warm blanket is a green, black, and blue** *plaid.*

plant-eat·er [plant'ēt'ər] *n.* An animal that eats only plants: **Cows are** *plant-eaters.*

pluck [pluk] *v.* To pull off or pull out: **Steve wanted to** *pluck* **some daisies from the field to give to his grandmother.**

plum·met [plum'it] *v.* **plum·met·ed, plum·met·ing** To fall straight down: **The wind had stopped, and the kite was** *plummeting* **toward the ground.**

plump [plump] *adj.* A little fat: **He bought a** *plump* **chicken to cook for dinner.**

port [pôrt] *n.* A place that ships come to and leave from: **The** *port* **was so small that there was room for only ten boats.** *syn.* harbor

prai·rie [prâr'ē] *n.* A large area of almost flat grassy land with no trees. *syn.* plain

pre·cious [presh'əs] *adj.* Worth a great deal of money; valued by someone: **The thief took only** *precious* **gems from the store, leaving less valuable jewelry behind.**

pre·serve [pri·zûrv'] *v.* To keep something in its original form: **A camper who cares about nature** *preserves* **the park by not littering and by putting out campfires carefully.**

pro·pel·ler [prə·pel'ər] *n.* Blades turned by a motor to move a boat or an airplane through water or air: **Both boats stopped when their** *propellers* **got caught in a huge fishing net.**

Q

qui·et [kwī′ət] *adj.* Making no noise: **Kenji liked to play music and sing when the house seemed too** *quiet.* *syn.* silent

R

re·ceiv·er [ri•sē′vər] *n.* The part of the telephone that you hold to your ear: **No voice came from the** *receiver* **of the telephone, so Mom hung up.**

rec·og·nize [rek′əg•nīz′] *v.* To know or to tell apart: **Hector and Ramon could** *recognize* **their sister even though she was wearing a mask.**

reef [rēf] *n.* A ridge of sand, rocks, or coral, away from the shore but close to the water's surface: **Juana went swimming off the** *reef* **so she could look at the pretty tropical fish and sea plants.**

re·mind [ri•mīnd′] *v.* **re·mind·ed, re·mind·ing** To help someone remember: **Alice** *reminded* **Benny which bus to take to her house even though he had been there twice before.**

re·trieve [ri•trēv′] *v.* To get and bring back: **The dog liked to** *retrieve* **the stick and drop it at Sarah's feet every time she threw it.**

rig·ging [rig′ing] *n.* The ropes used to raise and hold the sails of a ship: **The first time we attached the sail to the** *rigging,* **we put it on upside down!**

route [rōōt *or* rout] *n.* The way taken from one place to another: **The** *route* **of the school bus went past Carla's house.**

run·ner [run′ər] *n.* The long ski on the bottom of a sled used on snow and ice: **One** *runner* **on the bottom of the snowmobile looked crooked.**

recognize The word *recognize* has two main parts. *Re-* is a prefix that means "again" or "back." *Cognoscere,* a Latin word, means "to know." When you put the parts together, you can see that *recognize* means "to know again."

rigging

runner

a	add	ŏŏ	took
ā	ace	ōō	pool
â	care	u	up
ä	palm	û	burn
e	end	yōō	fuse
ē	equal	oi	oil
i	it	ou	pout
ī	ice	ng	ring
o	odd	th	thin
ō	open	th	this
ô	order	zh	vision

ə = { a in *above* e in *sicken*
      i in *possible*
      o in *melon* u in *circus* }

shammy A *shammy* is a smooth polishing cloth first made from the skin of an antelope. This animal lives in the mountains of France and has the French name *chamois* [sham•wä']. People who speak English have begun to spell the word s-h-a-m-m-y. You may see it spelled both ways in books written in English.

shrug

S

sal•vage [sal'vij] *n.* The act of saving something: **The team found many treasures during the *salvage* of the sunken ship.**

scat•ter [skat'ər] *v.* To spread out into different places: **Every time I tried to read the paper, the wind would *scatter* it all over the yard, and I would have to gather it up again.**

shad•ow [shad'ō] *n.* The shade or darkness made by something blocking light: **Playing in the sunny yard, Clara tried to step on Paco's *shadow*.**

shal•low [shal'ō] *adj.* Not deep: **The water was so *shallow* that it only came up to our ankles.**

sham•my [sham'ē] *n.* A soft leather made from the skin of antelopes or other animals: **Paula always used a *shammy* to polish her car.**

sharp•shoot•er [shärp'shoo'tər] *n.* Someone with very good aim: **Candace was such a *sharpshooter* that she could make a basket from anywhere on the court.**

shrug [shrug] *v.* **shrugged, shrug•ging** To raise the shoulders to show that you aren't sure about something.

sledge [slej] *n.* A big sled used to move heavy loads over snow and ice: **The ranger put the injured skier on a *sledge* to move him to the hospital.**

slen•der [slen'dər] *adj.* Thin: **The trunks of young trees are very *slender* compared with the trunks of older trees.**

smol•der [smōl'dər] *v.* **smol•dered, smol•der•ing** To burn slowly, making smoke but no flame: **The fire *smoldered* after they thought it was out, and it burst into flame later.**

snow·mo·bile [snō′mō·bēl′] *n.* A small sled, powered by a motor, that goes on snow: **We could drive the *snowmobile* when there was a lot of snow.**

spire [spīr] *n.* The pointed top of a building: **The lightning struck the *spire* of the town hall and knocked down the top half.**

spray [sprā] *n.* Tiny drops of water blowing in the air: **I love to sit in the front of the boat with the *spray* hitting my face and cooling me off.**

sprin·kle [spring′kəl] *v.* sprin·kled, sprin·kling To let fall in drops: ***Sprinkling* the lawn is one of my jobs.**

spy [spī] *v.* spied, spy·ing To see or catch sight of: **Mrs. Lopez *spied* the children running over the hill on their way home.**

stat·ue [stach′ōō] *n.* Something made of clay, wood, metal, stone, or other material to look like a person or animal: **Lenora liked to make clay *statues* of cats in her art class.**

stitch [stich] *n.* In sewing, a link of thread in a fabric that joins parts of the fabric together or joins two different fabrics together: **The blue *stitches* were noticeable on the white dress.**

string [string] *v.* strung, string·ing To attach one or more strings to something: **As a joke, Maura *strung* Cassie's guitar with fishing line instead of guitar string.**

sur·face [sûr′fis] *n.* The outside or top part of something: **The *surface* of the desk was smooth and shiny.**

swift [swift] *adj.* Very fast: **The waiter made a *swift* dive and caught the glass as it fell off the table.**

snowmobile

statue

a	add	o͝o	took
ā	ace	o͞o	pool
â	care	u	up
ä	palm	û	burn
e	end	yo͞o	fuse
ē	equal	oi	oil
i	it	ou	pout
ī	ice	ng	ring
o	odd	th	thin
ō	open	th	this
ô	order	zh	vision

ə = { a in *above* e in *sicken* i in *possible* o in *melon* u in *circus* }

talon The use of the word *talon* to mean "claw" came in a roundabout way. The Latin word *talus* means "ankle." Then it became *talo*, meaning "heel." In English the meaning became "heel of an animal" and eventually "the claw of a bird of prey."

talon

tiller

T

tal·on [tal'ən] *n.* The claw of a bird of prey: **The falcon swooped down and, in its sharp *talons*, grabbed the field mouse.**

taut [tôt] *adj.* Stretched tight: **Dad and I pulled the ropes *taut* so the tent would not fall down.**

ter·rain [tə·rān'] *n.* An area of land: **Since the *terrain* was rocky and dry, farmers would have a hard time growing crops there.**

tex·ture [teks'chər] *n.* The feel of a fabric: **My new jeans and shirt had rough *textures* until I washed them to make them soft.**

thong [thông] *n.* A thin strip of leather: **Campers often use a *thong* to tie things together because leather is very strong and easy to tie.**

thread [thred] *v.* **thread·ed, thread·ing** To wind through openings: **We saw our cousins *threading* their way through the crowd at the carnival.**

throt·tle [throt'(ə)l] *n.* A lever or pedal that helps an engine start and run: **He pulled on the *throttle* to start the boat.**

till·er [til'ər] *n.* A handle used to steer a boat: **Letting go of the *tiller* will make a boat spin in circles.**

tim·ber [tim'bər] *n.* A piece of wood: **The *timbers* of the ship had begun to rot, so the crew used new wood for the repairs.**

tow [tō] *v.* **towed, tow·ing** To pull with a rope or a chain: **Rob will watch while the tugboat is *towing* the big ship down the river.**

trans·late [trans·lāt′ *or* tranz′lāt] *v.* To change words and sentences from one language into another: **Teresa could** *translate* **what her teacher said into Spanish so that her mother could understand it.**

tri·um·phant [trī·um′fənt] *adj.* Feeling thrilled and happy about winning: **The** *triumphant* **soccer team gave the trophy to the school principal after the game.**

U

un·con·trolled [un′kən·trōld′] *adj.* Out of control; without order or limits: **The** *uncontrolled* **floods could not be stopped, and they destroyed the farmland.**

un·har·ness [un·här′nis] *v.* **un·har·nessed, un·har·ness·ing** To unfasten or make free: **The farmer** *unharnessed* **the horses and let them go.**

V

vau·de·ville [vôd′(ə•)vil *or* vōd′(ə•)vil] *n.* A show with many different acts: **The** *vaudeville* **show had many songs, jokes, and dances.**

ven·ture [ven′chər] *n.* Something to do that is somewhat dangerous and might not be successful: **The tourist's first** *venture* **into the jungle brought him in close contact with a snake.**

vig·or·ous·ly [vig′ər•əs•lē] *adv.* With a great deal of energy.

W

wood·land [wŏŏd′lənd] *n.* The forest.

worn [wôrn] *adj.* Damaged because of long use: **The** *worn* **curtains had rips in them.**

wrig·gle [rig′əl] *v.* **wrig·gled, wrig·gling** To squirm or twist like a worm. *syn.* wiggle

vaudeville Six hundred years ago in France, there was a town called Vau-de-Vire. The people who lived there were famous for writing funny songs. Somehow, the name for these songs changed to *vaudeville*. Americans borrowed this word and used it to mean a show made up of songs, dances, comedy, and even circus acts.

vigorously

a	add	ŏŏ	took
ā	ace	ōō	pool
â	care	u	up
ä	palm	û	burn
e	end	yōō	fuse
ē	equal	oi	oil
i	it	ou	pout
ī	ice	ng	ring
o	odd	th	thin
ō	open	th	this
ô	order	zh	vision

ə = { a in *above*   e in *sicken*
i in *possible*
o in *melon*   u in *circus* }

INDEX OF
TITLES AND AUTHORS

Page numbers in light print refer to information about the author.

Acknowledgments continued

Lothrop, Lee & Shepard Books, a division of William Morrow & Company, Inc.: Cover illustration by Jim LaMarche from *Mandy* by Barbara D. Booth. Illustration copyright © 1991 by Jim LaMarche. Cover illustration by Barbara Cooney from *Roxaboxen* by Alice McLerran. Illustration copyright © 1991 by Barbara Cooney.

Macmillan Publishing Company, a division of Macmillan, Inc.: Cover illustration by Lisa McCue from *Sebastian [Super Sleuth] and the Crummy Yummies Caper* by Mary Blount Christian. Illustration copyright © 1983 by Macmillan Publishing Company.

Margaret K. McElderry Books, an imprint of Macmillan Publishing Company: "Cricket and Mountain Lion" from *Back in the Beforetime: Tales of the California Indians*, retold by Jane Louise Curry. Text copyright © 1987 by Jane Louise Curry.

The Millbrook Press: Cover illustration by Jan Davey Ellis from *Mush!* by Patricia Seibert. Illustration copyright © 1992 by Jan Davey Ellis.

Morrow Junior Books, a division of William Morrow & Company, Inc.: Cover illustration from *Peter and the Wolf*, retold and illustrated by Michèle Lemieux. Copyright © 1991 by Michèle Lemieux. "The Crow and the Pitcher" from *Belling the Cat and Other Aesop's Fables*, retold by Tom Paxton, illustrated by Robert Rayevsky. Text copyright © 1990 by Tom Paxton; illustrations copyright © 1990 by Robert Rayevsky.

Pantheon Books, a division of Random House, Inc.: Cover illustration by Ann Strugnell from *The Stories Julian Tells* by Ann Cameron. Illustration copyright © 1981 by Ann Strugnell.

Philomel Books: *Owl Moon* by Jane Yolen, illustrated by John Schoenherr. Text copyright © 1987 by Jane Yolen; illustrations copyright © 1987 by John Schoenherr. *Lon Po Po, A Red-Riding Hood Story from China* by Ed Young. Copyright © 1989 by Ed Young.

Price Stern Sloan Publishers, Inc., Los Angeles, CA: "Chocolate Chip Cookie Caper" from *50 Mysteries I Can Solve* by Susannah Brin and Nancy Sundquist, illustration by Neal Yamamoto.

Random House, Inc.: Cover illustration by Keith Kohler from *The Titanic: Lost and Found* by Judy Donnelly. Illustration copyright © 1987 by Keith Kohler. Illustration from p. 62 by Arnold Lobel from *The Random House Book of Poetry for Children*, selected by Jack Prelutsky. Illustration copyright © 1983 by Random House, Inc.

Every effort has been made to locate the copyright holders for the selections in this work. The publisher would be pleased to receive information that would allow the correction of any omissions in future printings.

Photograph Credits

Key: (t) top, (b) bottom, (c) center.

Momatiuk/Eastcott/Woodfin Camp & Associates, 118(c); Caroline Povungnituk, *Untitled (Otter)*, ©1957, Stone, 6.9 x 19.3 x 8.2 cm, The Swinton Collection, Gift of the Women's Committee, Ernest Mayer/Winnepeg Art Gallery, 118–119(t); Paul McMormick/The Image Bank, 118–119(c); S. J. Krasemann/Peter Arnald, Inc., 119(t); Stephen J. Krassemann/Photo Researchers, 119(b); R. Bunge/Bruce Coleman, Inc., 206(t); Wendy Watriss/Woodfin Camp, 206(b); Luis Castanada/The Image Bank, 206–207(c); Ancient Art & Architecture Collection, 207(t); Tom McHugh/Photo Researchers, 207(c); Craig Lovell/Viesti Associates, 207(b); Nawrocki Stock Photo, 328–329; Peter A. Silva, 329(t)

Illustration Credits

Key: (t) top, (b) bottom, (c) center.

Table of Contents Art

Thomas Vroman Associates, Inc., 4, 5, 6, 7, 8, 9

Unit Opener Art

Thomas Vroman Associates, Inc., 10, 11, 120, 121, 208, 209

Bookshelf Art

Thomas Vroman Associates, Inc., 12, 13, 122, 123, 210, 211

Theme Opening Art

Mary M. Collier, 14–15; Sharron O'Neil, 66, 67; Linda Graves, 96, 97

Unit 2

John Jones 124, 125; Susan Keeter, 158, 159; Dom Lee, 182, 183

Unit 3

Cheryl Hanna, 212, 213; Nick Catalano, 262, 263; Loretta Lustig, 294, 295

Theme Wrap-up Art

Thomas Vroman Associates, Inc., 65, 95, 117, 157, 181, 205, 261, 293, 327

Connections Art

Sue Parnell, 119(b)

Selection Art

John Schoenherr, 16–31; Jim Arnosky, 32–45; Ann Strugnell, 46–57; Manuel Garcia, 59–64; Judy Labrasca, 98–115; Arnold Lobel, 116; Beatriz Vidal, 126–137; Jim Campbell, 138–139; Ed Young, 160–171; Robert Rayevsky, 174–175; Jennifer Hewitson, 176–180; Denise Brunkus, 184–201; Gordon Sauve, 204; Neal Yamamoto, 204; Jerry Pinkney, 214–243; Mr. Amos Ferguson, 246–247; Stephen Gammell, 248–259; Gail Gibbons, 264–283; Chris Van Allsburg, 296–319; Ken Brown, 322–326